CW01508654

SURVIVAL FIRST

THE REBEL ENTREPRENEUR'S GUIDE TO RISK, RICHES AND IMMORTALITY

ALEXANDER CARLOS CONCEPCION

PUBLISHING COMPANY

SURVIVAL FIRST

The Rebel Entreupreneur's Guide to Risk, Riches and Immortality

ISBN **979-8-9899385-2-0** *Hardcover*

979-8-9899385-1-3 *Paperback*

979-8-9899385-0-6 *Ebook*

979-8-9899385-3-7 *Audiobook*

Dedication

*To my dad, Carlos. You took me to my first bookstore and told me
I would never be bored once I learned to love books. You were right.
Imagine what it's like writing one.*

*To my mom, Lucy. Thanks for giving me more love than I know what
to do with.*

*To my sister, Christine. Thanks for being my big sister, saving me
money on taxes, and always betting on me.*

To my abuela, Teresita. Thanks for showing me how to use my voice.

*To the rebel, creator, and entrepreneur reading this.
Thank you for betting on yourself.*

This book is for all of you.

THROUGH DARKNESS, LIGHT

Contents

INTRODUCTION

All I wanted was to survive.

I was in the third year of running my real estate business when lockdowns began. Businesses everywhere were closing—small ones, big ones, old ones, new ones. Nobody seemed safe. Friends were losing everything. I was losing clients left and right before my big moneymaking season was set to begin. Sales would begin drying up soon.

I thought my business was next.

Before starting Taco Street Locating, I was living in a shitty apartment, eating cheap lentils, and asking Dad for rent money. Now I was making six figures, living in a nice downtown apartment, and ordering extra guacamole with everything. My business saved me from the simulated corporate reality of glass buildings, suits, ties, cubicles, office politics, Sunday scaries, fake friendships, working on stuff I didn't care about for people I didn't like, and letting my soul be molded into something optimized for shareholder value.

Having my own business meant never having to ask for time off. I owned my time. I could wake up whenever I wanted and do whatever I wanted. I could read books, hang out with friends, play disc golf, go on long walks, work out five times a week, book one-way tickets to Europe for months on end, and spend time with my family.

I was years past living with constant financial anxiety and the dread of professional aimlessness. Instead, I was making what felt like ridiculous amounts of money, providing a service people loved, watching my crazy ideas flourish, and living on my terms. More than anything else, I was learning what it was like to bet on myself and win.

Entrepreneurship was a one-way trip. It was the key to the life I wanted. I couldn't go back. Surviving meant everything. Now I was staring at the real possibility that everything I built might implode.

Luckily, my fears were way off. The pandemic kept spreading, but business roared back. Deep into lockdown, I was cranking out record-breaking month after record-breaking month. By the end of the year, my business had doubled in revenue. It was awesome...and confusing. Why was I doing so well when everyone around me seemed to be falling apart?

I had some vague ideas. I suspected some of it must have been my vast brilliance. I also suspected much of it had nothing to do with me. If my entrepreneurship-enabled freedom was going to last, I had to understand why my business had survived so that it could continue to survive—not for years but for decades. To do that, I needed to understand why my business wouldn't survive. I needed to understand risk.

Little did I know where this thought would take me. This tiny thought-seed blossomed into an ecosystem of thought. It consumed three years of reading, research, thinking, and writing. This journey challenged everything I understood about myself, my business, and what it meant to survive. It rewired my mental DNA and changed how I related to the world. It triggered a life crisis, sent me into therapy, and led to the birth of a new business.

It radicalized me.

Risk, I found, wasn't just the key to survival.
It was the key to everything.

MEET THE AUTHOR/YOUR ADVENTURE BUDDY: TACO STREET LOCATING

To get the most out of a business book, it's important to see its lessons applied to a real business. That's what we're going to do. I'm going to show you how I took not only my business—Taco Street Locating—but *myself* through the same journey you'll be taking.

Taco Street is the Austin, Texas-based real estate business I started in 2018. We specialize in a niche called apartment locating. It's a simple business: we help people find apartments to rent. Apartments pay us when our clients move into their buildings. (And yes, I will explain why I have a taco-themed real estate business and what that has to do with risk, but that's a topic for another chapter.)

In five years, we've done over $850,000 in revenue. I work between fifteen and thirty hours a week and have spent a year traveling the world. My team fluctuates between four and eight people. We've thrived in an industry where most fail, adapted to shifting markets, grown during the pandemic, and coasted through a recession. We've had near-fatal disasters, lost important team members, watched key marketing channels collapse, and dealt with floods of new people entering the market, broken technology, and cash-flow problems.

More than anything, Taco Street has become an expression of who I am. It has helped me uncover my brilliance, biases, and shortcomings. It's allowed me to travel the world and buy a house in my favorite neighborhood. It's brought me to the edge of burnout and challenged what it means for me to be an entrepreneur.

WHO THIS BOOK IS FOR

You are an entrepreneur because you can't be anything else. You can't live as a cog in someone else's dream. You are willing to suffer the trials, tribulations, and traumas of entrepreneurship so that you can build your own.

Maybe you're lone-wolfing it and running a business by yourself. Maybe you're the captain of a small, plucky band of entrepreneurial misfits conspiring to bring something great into the world. Maybe you're the pilot of a corporate airship looking to keep it from crashing into the side of a mountain. Whichever one you are, your fate is in your hands. Whether your business lives, dies, or thrives is up to you.

WHAT YOU'RE GOING TO GET

You are going to learn a radically new yet practical framework that I call the RDEE (pronounced "ardy") formula, which describes risk with three variables: damage, existence, and exposure. This formula sets a new foundation for making decisions that will help you survive and thrive as an entrepreneur. It will help you adapt to a world outside your control and build a more resilient business. Most importantly, it will show you how to navigate your role in your business. If you apply this framework to your business, you will learn how to avoid risks that would otherwise destroy you, and uncover opportunities that will make you rich.

HOW TO READ THIS BOOK

Part 1: The Risk Renaissance is the much-needed update on why and how to think about risk. There, I lay out the foundational concepts for the book. I shift risk away from the boring academic jargon you're used to toward a new kaleidoscopic worldview that will reframe how we approach not only survival but everything in your business. These chapters revolve around the following questions:

- Why focus on risk?
- What is survival?
- What is risk?
- What is the relationship between risk and opportunity?
- How do we experience risk?
- How do we detect risk, and what do we do about it?

The rest of the book is about applying the RDEE framework to your business. Each chapter follows a similar structure. I'll tell a story of a real-world business and explain what's at stake, what risks and opportunities exist, how to think about them, how to approach making decisions, and how I've applied the lessons to my business, Taco Street. Throughout the book, I will invite you to describe how the lessons apply to yourself and your business.

For most stories in this book, I've used the real names of entrepreneurs and their businesses. For others, I've anonymized the names because, well...people don't like to get sued. Parts 2, 3, and 4 flow from the external big picture to the internal little picture. Reading them in the order presented makes sense. However, with Part 1's foundation set, you can treat the rest as a Choose Your Own Adventure book and read each chapter in whichever order you'd like.

Part 2: External Risk is about risks you don't control. These chapters look at your industry, markets, economics, and politics. You'll learn to understand the environmental conditions that make your business possible, why those conditions might change, and how you can adapt to those changes.

Part 3: Internal Risk is about risks you do control. This section explores your business model, product-market fit, marketing, "competition," operations, legal issues, cybersecurity, and money. We'll tackle foundational business concepts such as what a business model is, what competition is (and if it's even real), and why the sitcom *I Love Lucy* is the key to understanding operations.

Part 4 is about the Ultimate Risk: you. We'll explore the most important issues, such as if you're competent enough, what happens when you're not around, what happens when you take too much from your business, and what happens when your business takes too much from you. We'll end by looking at your business's risk to you, the entrepreneur.

I will take you on the same journey I went through while reexploring risk and opportunity and discuss how to apply it to your reality. This book will force you to look at yourself and your business and ask simple but difficult questions. You will experience the tension of uncovering uncomfortable vulnerabilities, the relief of resolving them, and the excitement of discovering new opportunities hiding in plain sight.

Ready for the ride? Let's get started.

PART 1: THE RISK RENAISSANCE

I'm going to guess your initial reaction to the word *risk* is something like a kid's reaction to steamed broccoli—somewhere between disdain and apathy. Risk pairs with words like boring, dry, and complicated. If you're like most entrepreneurs I know, a part of you feels even thinking about risk summons misfortune. So you ignore it and move on with your life.

I understand. I was like that too...until I went down the risky rabbit hole.

What I discovered is that risk isn't merely the best way to understand how to survive, but how to think about everything in business. Risk is the sun all other subjects revolve around. Risk is the alpha and the omega.

I'll forgive your skepticism.

The problem is the way we've been taught to think about risk works for classrooms and boardrooms, but not for entrepreneurs like us.

Risk needs an update...a renaissance if you will.

Part 1: The Risk Renaissance distills risk down to a simple, relatable, and practical worldview that will help us find solutions to complex problems. Chapter 1 details why risk deserves the main-character role of this book. Chapter 2 looks at the relationship between risk and opportunity. Chapter 3 explores how we experience risk and introduces the question-based RDEE formula we will use throughout the book. Chapter 4 describes types of risks and how they manifest in the world. Chapter 5 introduces new words that will reframe how we tackle risk.

Ready to begin? Allow me to be the Virgil to your Dante and guide you through darkness into light.

CHAPTER 1

WHY DO BUSINESSES DIE?

FOR IMMEDIATE RELEASE

A Message from the CEO: Closure of [Company Name] Due to Unforeseen External Circumstances

Dear Valued [Customers, Employees, Partners, or Community]

It is with a heavy heart that I announce the closure of [Company Name]. As CEO, I want to personally explain the reasons behind this decision, which has been forced upon us by unforeseen external circumstances.

For years, [Company Name] has been dedicated to delivering [specific products or services] of the highest quality to our esteemed customers. We have strived to go above and beyond to ensure your satisfaction. Your loyalty and support have meant the world to us.

Regrettably, despite our unwavering commitment and tireless efforts, circumstances beyond our control have compelled us to make this difficult choice. [Brief explanation of the external circumstances, such as economic downturn, industry changes, regulatory challenges, or natural disasters] have severely impacted our ability to sustain our operations and fulfill our financial obligations.

I want to thank you for your understanding and support during this challenging time. We are profoundly grateful for the opportunity to have served you and for the trust you have placed in us.
Sincerely,
[Name]
CEO, [Company Name]

I'll give you a minute to puke in the corner.

This sad-violin public-relations-style business obituary is what ChatGPT spit out when I asked it for a business closing statement. If reading it made you cringe as much as it did me, it's because you've read nonsense like this a million times. It's annoying. The same people bull-horning to the world about how great their businesses are suddenly disappear behind the curtains of generic say-nothing statements when things go south.

When I started venturing to understand why my business was doing fine and others weren't, I started on local food blogs that wrote about restaurant openings and closings. I noticed a trend. New restaurants got full-length articles. Closings, if they got any mention at all, were announced with some variation of the public-relations word salad above. The more I dug, the more I saw the same pattern.

People love hearing about new and successful businesses. Successful entrepreneurs write books, become social media stars, go on podcasts, get full-length newspaper articles, and give keynote speeches at prestigious conferences. They credit their hard work, discipline, brilliance, resilience, self-belief, and commitment to things like service, customers, mission, and "culture." We don't hear about luck, low interest rates, favorable rules, perfect market conditions, or the wealthy networks they were born into.

Even most "failure" stories are really "how I failed before becoming successful" stories. Business obituaries paint the owners as valiant heroes victimized by external circumstances. Nobody talks about their broken business models, fragile marketing plans, crappy products, operational meltdowns, toxic gaslighting cultures, petty lawsuits, delusional growth projections, incompetent managers, reckless spending, egomaniacal owners, or people who simply lost the will to go on. Not once have I seen an entrepreneur go on a podcast tour after their business dies. How strange!

Even close friends of mine who shut their businesses down have glossed over the closure or quickly changed the subject when asked about it. One in particular told everyone about the hundreds of thousands of dollars he raised for his new business, but then, a few years later, things went south, and he shut down the business without even mentioning it. I had no idea until months later. It took some one-on-one time with heavy doses of steak and whiskey to get the full story.

The honest, self-reflective stories where people describe and take responsibility for their downfall are usually hidden deep in online forums written by anonymous authors. It was confusing. I couldn't understand why people weren't excited about broadcasting their most traumatic and humiliating professional experiences. Successful entrepreneurs, it seemed, talk to audiences. Failed entrepreneurs talk to therapists.

All business closure statistics tell slight variations of the underlying reality that most businesses close soon after opening. Yet nobody talks about why they close. Instead, these stories and lessons learned go quietly into an infinite ocean of unmarked graves. I figured that business owners had to be falling into predictable traps. I suspected the answer to why most businesses died lay in the wet-blanket word everyone acknowledged but nobody untangled: risk. Risk is the only business concept that directly addresses survival.

Entrepreneurs seem to focus on everything *but* risk. Sure, people say the word *risk* all the time, but I have never heard anyone even attempt to define it. For as big of a concept as risk is, nobody seems to want to touch it. Risk is the kid warning everyone about Monday morning's math exam on Friday night—in other words, the kid who's not invited to the party. Instead, the world is flooded with "content" about viral marketing schemes, persuasive copywriting, positive mindsets, hustle, grit, grind, manifesting, "personality studies," culture, morning routines, and habits. Some of it is useful. Most of it is garbage.

It isn't hard to understand why entrepreneurs ignore risk. Entrepreneurs are optimists who don't want to spend their lives thinking about bad stuff. But that's the problem. The people with the most risk are the last ones to think about it. Entrepreneurs seem to overlook something basic: nothing matters if you don't survive. Dead businesses don't grow, make products, launch marketing campaigns, form cultures, or change the world. Dead businesses don't do shit.

Here's the truth:
- Persuasive copywriting won't fix a bad product.
- Positive mindsets won't stop surprise lawsuits.
- Politicians don't care about your hustle, grind, and grit.
- Amazing products won't matter if your operations suck.
- Culture won't block cyberattacks.
- Manifesting won't fix a broken business model.
- Morning routines won't stop your best employee from leaving.
- Knowing your Myers–Briggs won't stop your business partners from bailing on you.

But understanding risk, I thought, might be the answer.

So where could I learn about risk? Business school didn't help me. My finance and economics degrees were résumé fodder for big conglomerates and had nothing to do with running a small business. Harvard MBA–type case studies are bone-dry fact patterns that ignore the emotional roller coaster entrepreneurs experience. Any risk-related business course teaches abstract jargon and complex formulas to people pursuing academia or the risk departments of large corporations. No business owner I've known has had a risk department or a PhD in math or has used complex risk formulas. If the pandemic taught me anything, it is that no ordinary person calculates risk with formulas. Besides, how would we even track risk? I've never heard anyone brag about how they reduced risk by 30 percent. Risk is more about what *didn't* happen than about what did.

Business books aren't much better. Most are self-congratulatory success-porn narratives written by personality cultists, academics applying misinterpreted pop psychology, marketers shilling get-rich-quick schemes, and gurus offering prescriptive success formulas without the context to be useful. Rare exceptions are authors like Nassim Taleb and Daniel Kahneman, who look at risk from refreshing historical, psychological, mathematical, and even religious perspectives that are digestible by even a simpleton like me. Still, their work is too disconnected from what I was looking for.

When researching risk, I couldn't find anyone describing it in a way that mapped to my reality as a small entrepreneur. I don't have a risk department, lobbyists, venture financing, or mass datasets to plug into fancy PhD-level formulas. I am the captain of a small ship, responsible for everything. I picked my industry and where I do business. It's my job to adapt to a world I don't control. I choose how I make money, where I market, how I present myself, the services I offer, the clients I work with, who I hire and fire, what tools I use, and what I spend money on. I am responsible for the emotions I am and am not experiencing. For better and worse, my fate is in my hands. To understand risk, I realized I would have to learn about how it applied to my business by myself.

So I got morbid. I searched for every entrepreneurial horror, disaster, obituary, and near-death story out there. I scoured the internet, read books, listened to podcasts, and plucked stories out of reluctant friends. I figured the better I understood what *not* to do, the better I'd understand what to do.

The more stories I found, the more patterns I saw. Things went wrong for all sorts of reasons, but they all seemed to be variations of predictable problems. The tragedy was how obvious things seemed in hindsight after it was too late. Sometimes problems were outside the entrepreneur's control. Sometimes problems were inside their control, but they ignored them. Always it was the entrepreneur at the center—whether they admitted it or not.

I reflected these lessons onto myself and my business. Over time, things started to make more sense. The root of the problem wasn't just the bad decisions people were making. Broken foundational concepts at the core of business were leading to bad decisions. I had to look at the foundation of my business to find what I was looking for.

Risk as a logical concept that can be described with numbers and formulas makes sense for banks and insurance companies but is absurd for ordinary people like me. I didn't have a formula that calculated the odds my business partner would quit after divorcing his wife, and how much money I would lose as a result.

How people experience and act on risk is obviously emotional. Anybody who watched people freak out during the pandemic could see that. The same has to be true in business. How we experience and make decisions around risk is more emotional than logical.

The more I thought about risk, the more I saw a deeper problem. The default phrases, words, and concepts we use around risk don't match our realities. Instead, we inherited a vocabulary from a time when small, internet-enabled entrepreneurs like me didn't exist. Words like *risk*, *failure*, and *survival* float around as unexamined abstract concepts. This leads to vague and ultimately broken frames that lead to bad decisions and bad outcomes.

I needed to deconstruct and rebuild those concepts in ways I could relate to. Over time, I built a new foundation that reshaped how I think about everything. I found myself reconstructing basic ideas like business models, economics, marketing, and competition. I even changed my vocabulary around risk.

The most radical shift came when I discovered the relationship between risk and opportunity. Understanding one meant understanding the other. Understanding both together unlocked a frame that seemed to perfectly describe the central tension at the heart of the entrepreneurial experience.

This journey rewired my emotional and logical DNA and changed how I relate to the world. Reflections on my business became reflections on myself. I stumbled on truths both painful and exciting. I didn't get this far with scientific studies, pop psychology, complex math, or Harvard MBA–style case studies. I found everything I needed in readily observable truths, simple logic, and relatable stories from ordinary entrepreneurs.

This book is a result of that journey. At its core, this book is a guide on surviving and thriving in a world of uncertainty. It is the book I wish I would have had when I started out as an entrepreneur.

KEY TAKEAWAYS

- Your first job as an entrepreneur is to survive. Nothing else matters if you don't.

- Most businesses don't survive, but most of their stories go untold.

- Understanding how risk relates to you means changing the words and frames that we use to think about it.

CHAPTER 2

RISK AND OPPORTUNITY

I spent the first two years after college getting rejected from countless job interviews. I lived at home with my parents, despairing about where my life was—or wasn't—going. This wasn't how I imagined starting out life in the "real world." I was desperate for something—anything—to happen, but it wasn't going to happen living at home.

I needed a blank slate. A reset. So I did the most rational thing I could think of: I burned my college diplomas. This was practically worthless but spiritually necessary to derail myself from the path those diplomas would have set me on.

"I'm moving to Austin, Texas," I told my parents while we sat for dinner.

As good parents, they were concerned.

"Did you get a job there?" Dad asked.

"No," I said.

"What about money?" Mom asked.

"I've got, uh...about $1,500." It was all I had. Moving was risky. I needed to find a job fast, or I would go broke, have to run back to Mom and Dad's, and plunge further into despair.

But I sensed an opportunity. Austin seemed cool; its economy was exploding, and swarms of smart people were flocking there. If I was going to dive into the unknown, Austin seemed like the right place to do it. Besides, I didn't have *that* much to lose. I was single, careerless, and had no family to support.

So I packed my car and drove off. There, I set in motion the series of events that would lead me to become the entrepreneur, and now author, I am today. Eight years later, I can say it was the best decision I ever made.

WHAT IS RISK?

Risk is potential bad stuff. You already knew that. But you probably haven't unpacked the three concepts inside that definition: *potential*, *bad*, and *stuff*.

Potential is stuff we don't know is going to happen. Uncertainty is inherently neutral. How we experience it depends on our relationship to the outcome. A team winning the Super Bowl is great for one set of fans and terrible for the other. Even a seemingly terrible thing like a pandemic can be great if you're the kind of business that profits from it.

Uncertainty is the default state of reality. We never know what's going to happen. This is why entrepreneurship is such a mindfuck. Surviving requires making the right set of decisions with unknown outcomes in a complex world that is always changing in unknown ways.

Bad is a negative. It's anything you don't want to happen.

Stuff is the most important part of our "potential bad stuff" definition of risk. *Stuff* is what we're protecting.

To understand risk, we need to first understand survival.

WHAT IS SURVIVAL?

Let's first describe what survival isn't. It's not failure. Businesses don't "fail." This isn't school. There is no arbitrary pass/fail number that determines whether you succeed or fail. Businesses don't get knocked out either. Nothing, outside maybe armed intervention, forces you to shut down.

Businesses *tap out.* More specifically, the people behind the businesses tap out. Your business dies when *you* decide you don't want to do it anymore. *Survival is choosing to not tap out.* Risk is whatever makes you want to tap out and stop being an entrepreneur. Everyone has different motives for tapping out, but they fall into three categories: money, time, and energy.

Money

Money is the obvious one. You're not a charity. You wouldn't be in business if you weren't making money. But of the three elements, money is the least important. Your business doesn't immediately shut down when your bank account hits zero. Money is infinite. You can earn it, borrow it, and raise it.

Time

You *do* need time to make money. You can't run a business if you don't have time to run a business. Time is finite. You also want time for your personal life. You probably won't want to run your business if you have no time for your life outside the business.

Energy

But money and time aren't enough. You can have all the time and money in the world, but you won't have a business if you don't have the energy to do it. Energy is the most important resource. It's whatever makes you want to do business. Energy includes the surface stuff you tell other people, like making money, solving problems, and saving the world.

But at its core, energy is emotional. It's the *excitement* of making money, the *thrill* of making cool shit with people you like, the *love* of pursuing your passion, the *freedom* of owning your time, the *relief* of avoiding financial anxiety, the *satisfaction* of helping people, and the *fulfillment* of executing a vision.

Energy is also the shadowy stuff you'd rather not admit, such as greed, status, power, and validation.

Negative emotions drain your energy. It's the *fear* of going broke, the *stress* of making payroll, the *disappointment* of firing someone, the *rage* from getting screwed out of a deal, the *frustration* of dealing with government bureaucracies, the *exhaustion* of working too hard, the *sadness* of broken relationships, and the *depression* of watching things go wrong. It's also the loss of health and the feeling of spending time away from people you love.

So when we talk about bad stuff happening, risk is about lost money and time, but most importantly, it's about the negative emotions we experience. If your business turns your life into a nonstop shitshow of "god-fucking-dammit," you probably won't want to do it anymore, no matter how much money it makes. This means that the core of risk isn't about logic, numbers, or formulas—but *emotions*.

Take some time to describe what survival means to you. This is the bare minimum it takes for you to keep being an entrepreneur. How much money do you need? What's the maximum amount of time you're willing to put in? What would make you want to tap out? Once you define what survival means to you, then you can better understand what you're protecting.

So that's risk: the bad cop. Now let's meet the good cop: opportunity.

WHAT IS OPPORTUNITY?

The test of a first-rate intelligence is the ability to hold two opposing ideas in mind at the same time and still retain the ability to function.
—F. Scott Fitzgerald

You're an entrepreneur. You're not here merely to survive. You're not playing *not to lose*. You're playing to *win*. That's why you'd rather think about everything other than risk.

If you don't think about risk, you won't get to play the game for long. But drinking too much Risk Kool-Aid isn't fun, practical, or even healthy. Overdosing on risk will extinguish your entrepreneurial energy, suffocate your upside, and spiral you into a totally-not-fun, depressive anxiety disorder. Ask me how I know.

The antidote is risk's inverse: opportunity. If risk is potential bad stuff, then opportunity is potential good stuff. Understanding both isn't just nice; it's necessary.

Take a scenario where you could lose $10,000. You'd be like, "Uh, fuck that." You'd focus on not losing that $10,000. However, if the scenario was you could lose $10,000 but gain $100,000, you'd be like, "Fuck that $10,000! I'll lose $20,000 if I can get that $100,000." This is asymmetry: the observation that outside ordinary coin flips, there is always an imbalance between upside and downside.

That's why understanding risk and opportunity together is so important. You'll make different decisions when you only see risk versus when you see risk *and* opportunity together. The core of this book's framework is learning to balance both so that you can make decisions that will make you rich while avoiding things that will destroy you. Throughout this book, we're going to flip frames from the negative (risk) to the positive (opportunity). Balancing this tension is the key to surviving and thriving.

This balance is easier said than done. As F. Scott Fitzgerald alludes to with his quote, the challenge is holding two opposing thoughts and emotions while keeping your shit together. Notice when you swing too much toward risk or opportunity. Darkness and light are both blinding. Reality is in between. Sober up wild optimism with realistic risk analysis. Imagine exciting opportunities to get yourself out of paralytic pessimism.

The problem is that life never gives us clear scenarios like the one above. Nor does it factor in lost time or the emotional complexities underneath. We have to discover our risks and opportunities on our own.

KEY TAKEAWAYS

· Survival is a choice. You choose to survive as an entrepreneur or not.

· Survival requires money, time, and—most importantly—the emotional energy to keep on going.

· Risk is the key to survival.

· Understanding risk is the key to understanding opportunity.

· Learning to balance risk and opportunity is the path to surviving and thriving.

CHAPTER 3

SENSING RISK

Soon after moving to Austin, I found a job inside the operations department of a fast-growing startup. I was an "implementation specialist," which basically meant entry-level data grunt. All in all, life was good, especially given how broke I was when I made the move. The work was tedious but simple. The hours were reasonable. I made enough money to pay rent and go out on weekends with friends and still have some left over.

The company was growing like wildfire. Every week, it seemed, the owners announced some new broken record, big new investment, market opening, or wave of new employees. I was strapped to a moneymaking rocket ship. My manager commented how lucky we all were, being on the ground floor of such an exciting company. He had a point. I had a stable job making decent money at a company where the equity I was vesting could be worth a lot in a few years. For the first time in my professional life, I was safe.

But I sensed something was off. Every time I heard "more," I felt worse. More growth meant more work, which meant more mindless clicky-clacking, more obnoxious CLANGALANGALANGINGS of the office phones, more drawn-out company meetings, and more calls with customers dumping meaningless problems on me.

Could I really do this for four years—the time it would take for my equity to fully vest? Could I handle years of impatiently waiting for the clock to strike five? Could I tolerate weekends of anxiety-dense

Sunday scaries? Was I going to let some human resources manager dictate when I could and couldn't see my family? Was I going to spend my life building simulated corporate relationships with internally dead coworkers? Was I going to wait until my thirties to accept I was on a false path?

Fuck no.

I was on the path to life on someone else's terms. Maybe that was fine for someone else, but not me. Nobody was going to give me the life I wanted. I was going to have to create it myself. I put in my notice a few weeks before my first equity phase was set to vest. It was a huge risk. I had no backup plan, no other job offers, and only a few months of savings. But the only thing riskier for me was not quitting.

That was seven years ago. Since then, I've made close to a million dollars and have still yet to ask anybody for time off.

RISK BLINDNESS

Everyone experiences survival the same. We'd all rather survive than not survive. But for reasons too complex for this book, relating to our biology, personality, upbringing, and experiences, we all experience risk differently.

What matters is how we act on risk. Sometimes we like it. Sometimes we don't. The difference depends on how we feel about uncertainty. When uncertainty excites us, we choose more risk. When it scares us, we choose less.

How we relate to risk explains the decisions we make: where we go (or don't) to college, where we live, the restaurants we dine at, the places we travel, the ways we spend money, the jobs we take and quit, the people we date and break up with, and the ways we build our businesses all depend on how we experience uncertainty.

What about you? Reflect on when you've chosen certainty over uncertainty and uncertainty over certainty—and why you made those decisions.

The tricky thing is that we're not consistent. Seemingly risk-loving people sometimes act paranoid. Seemingly paranoid people take wild risks. A skydiver may be fine with jumping out of planes but too afraid to quit their day job. Someone too afraid to leave their house in a pandemic may be the same person going half a million dollars in debt for a useless degree. The bold venture capitalist bro may be too afraid to talk to girls at a party. The bet-my-life-savings-on-cryptocurrency fanatic may be too afraid to take out a bank loan. The weekend drunk driver may be the one hoarding guns and ammunition for the coming apocalypse.

The problem with how we experience risk is when how we feel about risk doesn't match reality. I call this **risk blindness.**

Risk blindness makes big risks seem invisible and non-risks seem dangerous. The same goes for opportunity: **opportunity blindness** makes small opportunities seem huge and huge opportunities seem invisible. Risk blindness explains why we fall into predictable traps and ignore opportunities hiding in plain sight.

Risk blindness comes from a few places. Anybody who gets sweaty palms on a turbulent flight knows the disconnect between logic and emotion. When things get bumpy, we logically know we'll be fine, but our bodies aren't buying it. It's silently praying to any god that will listen. Biology doesn't help either. Our biology was built to protect us from tigers and dinosaurs, not bad business models and lawsuits. A bad business model won't freak us out the way a roach crawling on our leg will, but it will leave us broke.

Sometimes our biology works against us. The impulse that makes us want to fit into groups is the same drive that leads to us build bland, commoditized businesses that can't survive in a crowded market.

But more than anything else, risk blindness comes from false certainty.

That deal is *definitely* going through. That client is *definitely* going to pay me on time. My business partner *definitely* isn't a vindictive psychopath. That launch is *definitely* going to go well. That stock is *definitely* going up. My publisher *definitely* won't go out of business. I *definitely* won't get hit with some sudden lawsuit or tax bill. The company I'm partnering with *definitely* won't implode out of nowhere. There *definitely* won't be some world-changing pandemic. We're *definitely* going to keep growing. My employees *definitely* would never try to embezzle company funds. I'll *definitely* never get hacked.

How many times have you seen your assumptions broken? What were the consequences? If it could happen then, it can happen now.

Recklessness and paranoia aren't opposites; they're inverse expressions of the same sense of certainty. Reckless people are *certain* the risk doesn't exist, doesn't apply to them, or won't be that bad. Paranoid people are *certain* the risk does exist, and it's definitely going to happen—and the consequences will be terrible.

So what do we do?

ENTER THE RISK SENSE

Senses help us survive. We have a nose, a tongue, eyes, and ears to help us detect things that will harm or help us. What I propose is developing a new sense that will help us do the same for business. I call this the **risk sense.**

The risk sense isn't about becoming emotionally detached, risk-calculating automatons like Spock from *Star Trek*. Instead, the risk sense maps to the reality that we're responsible for creating businesses capable of surviving in the real world while protecting the emotional energy required to do it. Therefore, the risk sense combines rationally processing and emotionally connecting to risk.

Good risk sense will change how we experience reality and improve how we make decisions. Things that seemed risky, like launching that new product or hiring that extra employee, won't seem risky anymore. Things that seemed safe or innocuous, like your business model, marketing strategy, agreements with business partners, or daily schedule will seem deadly.

Developing your risk sense starts with delaying certainty, which creates the space for you to apply frames and questions that will stress and strengthen your assumptions. This is how you'll avoid the landmines that could destroy you, and discover the gold mines that will make you rich.

THE RDEE FORMULA

I did something crazy. I made a risk formula. This isn't some abstract numerical formula that attempts to boil down reality into numbers. That might work for physics, but not us. This formula reflects our lives, which involve complex dynamic circumstances and emotions. It's based on three simple questions that you can continually ask in order to discover your risks.

This is the **RDEE formula** (pronounced "ardy"):

Risk = Damage x Existence x Exposure

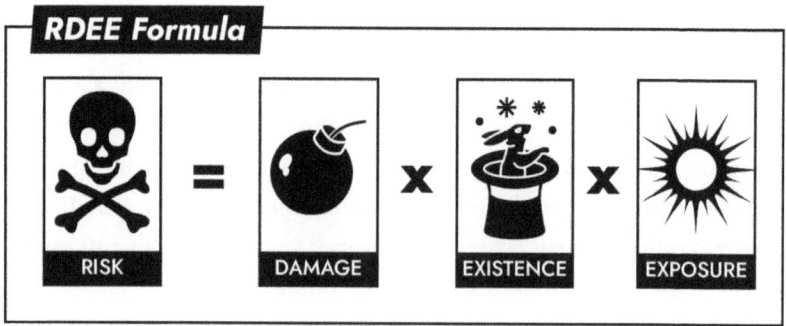

This formula is based on three questions.

Damage: What's at stake? Damage is the money, time, and—most importantly—emotional energy lost when something goes wrong. Damage can be a little or a lot.

Existence: What risks exist? Risks either exist or they don't.

Exposure: How likely will the risk happen? Either it's likely or unlikely. Let's take it out for a spin.

It's Saturday morning, and you're nestled comfortably on your couch primed for a multi-hour slate of Saturday-morning cartoons. On the table in front of you sits a bowl of tasty breakfast cereal.

Risk: The bowl falls off the table.

Damage: What happens if that bowl falls off? That depends.

Scenario 1: It's an empty bowl that falls on well-sealed hardwood flooring. You shrug it off, refill the bowl, and resume watching as if nothing happened. *Damage: low.*

Scenario 2: It's a ceramic bowl that falls and breaks on carpet flooring.

Mom takes five dollars from your weekly allowance. You spend the next ten minutes cleaning up the mess while feeling like a big dumb idiot, but life goes on. *Damage: mild.*

Scenario 3: It's your grandmother's heirloom crystal vase filled with rare, limited edition Cap'n Crunch. The vase falls and shatters into a million pieces, spilling milk all over Dad's favorite cowhide rug. Mom cancels your allowance. You are grounded for a million years. You sob uncontrollably as Dad breaks the TV and ruins Saturday-morning cartoons forever. *Damage: extreme.*

Existence: Because there is a bowl of cereal on the table, there exists a chance it will fall off the table. If there were no bowl on the table, there would be no chance of it falling off.

Exposure: That depends where the bowl is. The closer to the middle of the table it is, the lower the odds it falls. The closer to the edge, the higher the odds.

Risk and opportunity are inverses. So are their formulas.

Opportunity = Upside x Existence x Exposure

As before, let's take it out for a spin.

It's Friday morning, which means you're ignoring work and planning your weekend activities. You've received two invitations. The first is to chill with the homies and play beer pong. The second is to be a last-minute add-on to a retreat at an epic national park with a group of strangers.

Opportunity: You can have a great weekend.

Upside: This depends on which choice you make.

Scenario 1: You ignore both invites and watch Netflix all weekend. You're entertained by the curious lives of chimps and spooky serial killers. You have a pleasant weekend but feel dead inside come Sunday evening. *Upside: low.*

Scenario 2: You grab a thirty-pack of Natty Light and chill with the homies. You engage in satisfying banter, win some come-from-behind beer pong games, and go home with your friend's attractive coworker. *Upside: pretty good.*

Scenario 3: You say fuck it and go on the retreat. You explore epic terrains, turn strangers into lifelong friends, and discover your life's true calling. *Upside: mind-blowing.*

Existence: Your couch and Netflix account exist; therefore, you can sit at home and do nothing. Invitations to chill with the homies and go on the retreat exist. If there were no invitations, there'd be no opportunities.

Exposure: That depends on how easy it is to pick any option. Netflix at home costs next to nothing, so it's more likely to happen. Chilling with the homies costs some beer money and a quick drive, so it's also likely to happen. The retreat costs a lot of time, money, and energy, so it's the least likely to happen.

As we move on, take a moment to acknowledge a business risk or opportunity that keeps popping up in your head. Take the RDEE formula out for a spin. Describe the risk or opportunity. What's at stake? What risks or opportunities exist? How likely is it?

KEY TAKEAWAYS

· Pay attention to when uncertainty scares and excites you. This determines your relationship to risk and influences how you make decisions.

· Invisible risks and opportunities hide in bad assumptions. Always be prepared to challenge your assumptions.

· Risk is both rational and emotional. The questions proposed by the RDEE formula—What's at stake? What risks exist? How likely are those risks?—are the key questions we'll keep asking in order to detect risk.

CHAPTER 4

BECOMING A RISK SOMMELIER

The first step of the twelve-step Alcoholics Anonymous program is admitting you have a problem. You can't solve a problem if you won't admit there is a problem. The same applies to risk.

The first step in addressing risk is admitting you have a risk. This is the hardest step. As an entrepreneur, you are an optimist by necessity. Thinking about risk isn't fun or sexy. It's that feeling you get when Mom tells you to go to the dentist for the twentieth time. You know you should, but you'd rather not. So you put it out of your mind.

It feels better living in the safe, comfortable delusion, pretending everything is fine. But today's delusion is tomorrow's disaster. The risks I'm talking about are the ones your mind tries to shove to the back and ignore. But they don't go away. They keep resurfacing until either you accept them voluntarily or reality forces you to confront them. You can do it the easy way and listen to Mom or do it the hard way and wait until you start writhing in agonizing tooth pain.

Admitting a risk is the first step, but it isn't enough. We have to understand risk and its nuances in order to better act on it. For that we'll look toward the last people AA members want to be around: wine sommeliers.

Wine sommeliers are magicians. They can tell you anything about a wine—from its grape variety to region of origin and how many Instagram followers its makers have—merely by sniffing it. We're aiming to be like that, but for risk.

Risk sommeliers are also magicians. They can assess complex situations and make effective decisions that will create more riches than headaches. The risk sommelier is vigilant, not paranoid. Bold, not reckless. In groups, the risk sommelier will be both the person popping other people's overly optimistic balloons and the one pointing out opportunities others don't see.

Becoming a risk sommelier starts with learning the **risk flavors**.

THE RISK FLAVORS

Risk flavors are the different ways risks manifest in the real world, each with its own frames and questions that will help us understand the nature and severity of what we're dealing with so we can make better decisions.

Let's dip our noses into the glass of risk and sniff its varieties.

Ordinary risk is stuff you can imagine, like an employee quitting, a business deal falling through, a client leaving, or your laptop breaking.

Ordinary risks are the "best" risks. If you can imagine something, you can do something about it.

Black swan risk, borrowed from Nassim Taleb's book of the same name, describes stuff you never imagined happening. The logic goes like this: all your life, you've only seen white swans; therefore, you assume all swans must be white. Then one day you see a black swan. Something you never imagined is right there in front of you.

In business, a black swan can be a lot of things: a surprise lawsuit, getting hacked, a new technology that makes your business obsolete, losing a key business partner, an employee embezzling business funds, some stupid pandemic, or anything else you never saw coming. These are the most dangerous risks because you can't prepare for something you don't imagine.

The caveat is that a black swan is relative to the person experiencing it. For example, somebody who studies pandemics would have experienced the COVID-19 pandemic as an ordinary risk. This is why imagination is so important to approaching risk. Pairing your imagination with the right set of questions turns what would have been dangerous black swan risks into approachable ordinary risks.

Domino risk is what happens after something happens. Domino risk is important because it forces you to ask the follow-up question: *and then what?*

Domino 1: Your assistant quits. *And then what?*
Domino 2: You take on their tasks. *And then what?*
Domino 3: You work more hours trying to replace them. *And then what?*
Domino 4: You get frustrated, make less money, and burn out. *And then what?*
Domino 5: You shut down the business.

Domino risk sums up the consequences of each fallen domino. In this example, your assistant quitting leads to you shutting down the business. The caveat here is that it's easier to predict the second and third dominos than it is the subsequent dominos.

Compound risk isn't about one thing happening but many. You get hit with a lawsuit, *and* your best employee leaves, *and* you get hit with a surprise tax bill. Compound risk demonstrates why it's important to take seemingly small risks seriously. While each risk alone may be survivable, together they might be lethal. Think about this as death by a thousand risks. Compound risk will be a key player in the Operations Risk chapters.

Transfer risk is adopting third-party risks. For example, you run a marketing agency for venture-backed startups. If they go out of business, you lose your clients. Their risks become your risks. Or you have a barber shop in 1960s Detroit. All of your customers work in the auto industry. If the auto industry crashes, your customers lose their jobs, and they can't afford to pay you. Therefore, you take on the auto industry's risks. Or you use fancy sales software. The software company goes out of business. You lose your sales software. Their risks become your risks.

Transfer risk will play a critical role in Part 2: External Risk because it challenges you to think about the risks of the world around you rather than those inside of your business.

Timing risk isn't about what happens but when. Say you run a holiday store where most of your money comes between November and January. Losing your best employee will hurt you more during peak season than if they leave in the offseason. Timing risk is about seeing risk as a dynamic force that changes in severity.

Concentration risk is when one bad thing affects lots of things. All your business comes from Instagram ads. If Instagram shuts down your account, your entire business is affected. Only one of your employees knows how to do that super-important task. When they leave, you're screwed. Or all of your business comes from foot traffic in one neighborhood. Or most of your money comes from a single client. Or the most important ingredient for your food truck comes from a single supplier.

Middle risk is the most distinct risk. Here the danger isn't at the extremes; it's somewhere in the middle. What makes middle risk dangerous is that it seems innocuous. It's the product launch people like but don't love. It's the somewhat pleasing restaurant you won't go back to. It's the semi-incompetent employee you don't fire soon enough. It's the seven-out-of-ten relationship you stay in for years longer than you should.

THE OPPORTUNITY FLAVORS

Each risk flavor applies to an opportunity in the same way.

Ordinary opportunities are those you can imagine, like hiring a new assistant, opening in a new market, or launching a new product.

Black swan opportunities could be serendipitous events, like meeting the perfect business partner or launching a marketing campaign that goes viral out of nowhere.

Concentrated opportunities are like having a ton of money in a single investment that shoots up in price, or having a monopoly in the right market.

Domino opportunities are like the series of connections you make after attending a networking event or the word-of-mouth referrals you get after working with a client.

Transfer opportunities could be when a big new corporate headquarters opens up in your neighborhood and floods your coffee shop with new customers.

Compound opportunities are when a bunch of good things happen around the same time.

Timing opportunities are like when you open your store in a neighborhood right before the neighborhood becomes popular.

Middle opportunities are what comes from balancing two opposing forces, like when you pair the right product developer with the right marketer.

Discovering your risks and opportunities is ultimately about having the curiosity to ask good questions and the courage to answer them.

Take a few minutes to pick one or two "flavors" listed in this chapter and describe how they relate to your business.

Going through this process will suck as you inevitably stumble on uncomfortable realities. This process might also uncover exciting opportunities you never would have thought of otherwise. But sensing your risks and opportunities is only the first step. Now it's time to do something about it.

KEY TAKEAWAYS

· The first step to risk and opportunity is acknowledging they exist.

· Becoming a risk sommelier is about learning how to connect to risks and opportunities both rationally and emotionally.

· Ask the questions proposed by the risk flavors to put risks and opportunities in proper context so you can begin to make better decisions.

CHAPTER 5

WHAT TO DO ABOUT RISK

Brad Larsen is a doer. When he says he's going to do something, he does it. When he decided to quit his job and travel the world, he dropped everything and tore through forty countries in three years. When he decided to race triathlons, he did it—twenty times. After so much *doing,* Brad sensed what he really needed to do was...less.

That's when a sensory deprivation chamber entered his picture. These are enclosed chambers filled with dense saltwater where people can float, cut off from all senses. "I thought it was some hippie-dippie bull-shit," Brad said, "but I gave it a shot. I went in for my first float session, laid down in the salty water, closed my eyes...and woke up ninety minutes later. I've never felt so relaxed and clear-headed."

But it was more than that. Brad's float was like Moses downloading the Ten Commandments atop Mount Sinai. It was a revelation. Brad sensed more than just a business opportunity—he sensed a mission. So Brad did what Brad does: he went all in. He was hell-bent on getting his own float tank business. That was when Float Temple was conceived.

Brad raised some money from friends and family and recruited two business partners. Business Guy was Brad's best friend who brought corporate business experience to the table. Money Guy had a ton of money from successful investments. This entrepreneurial triumvirate would bring Float Temple to life.

With plans, financing, operating agreements, and real estate secured, they were ready to go. "We'll be open in six months no problem!" Brad thought.

What followed was a jungle gym of bureaucratic red tape, permitting issues, and incompetent contractors. "We were delayed a week because the fucking *screw inspector* was on vacation." Delays cost them over $40,000 in lost rent.

Eventually, Float Temple opened. "The Float Temple is where you recharge and discover the infinite energy within you," the mission statement read.

Float Temple was a three-man team, but it became a one-man show. Business Guy didn't want to be involved in running the business. Money Guy, despite having plenty of money himself, didn't want to spend it. "I had to get approval for anything over $500," Brad fumed.

For someone who wanted to do less, Brad did a lot. "I never stopped working. I cleaned, marketed, wrote emails, served customers, hired, fired, managed contractors, fought with bureaucrats, and handled all administrative work." With his small salary, he lived like a monk in a shoebox studio above Float Temple.

One business problem surprised him: "You can't control who walks into brick-and-mortar spaces. There are some psychos out there, man. You'd be shocked at what people are willing to threaten in order to get a $20 discount."

It took longer than expected, but Float Temple eventually stabilized. "Things were getting good. We had a good team, became profitable, and I could finally afford groceries," Brad said.

And then the pandemic began.

"The mask police would regularly give us citations for being open, but we *had* to be open. We couldn't just *not* make money. We basically became a speakeasy in order to survive."

It wasn't all bad. "Float Temple's community was amazing. I met some awesome people and made great friends. I don't know how I could have made it without them." One perk, of course, was getting to float as much as he wanted. "Float Temple was the cause of and solution to all of my problems," Brad recalls, laughing at the paradox.

After a few years, the relationships between the partners began deteriorating. Business Guy and Money Guy blamed Brad for not making enough money. Brad blamed them for not being involved. What followed was a complex tangle of handshake agreements, renegotiations, and threats until things hit a breaking point.

Business Guy and Money Guy tapped out. They were done with Float Temple and put their equity up for sale. Despite everything, Brad wanted to keep going. They made it through the pandemic alive. Things were getting good. "We were profitable again. We had good employees and a strong community."

But unable to buy out his partners, Brad had to sell Float Temple. "Fire-selling Float Temple to a bunch of Canadians looking for visas was not on my bingo board. Going through it was awful. I put so much work into it for it to end like this. I maxed out my credit cards and even considered bankruptcy. My best friend became my former best friend. The worst part was the loneliness. Inside I was going through absolute hell and couldn't let anyone know. Fortunately, I was able to pay back my friends and family most of the money they invested."

After the dust settled, for the first time in a long time, Brad had time to slow down and reflect. "I needed to go through this. I had a vision and fought to bring it to life. It was hard, terrible, amazing, and the most profound experience of my life."

WHAT TO DO ABOUT RISK

So far, we've looked at why risk is a big deal and how to sense it. Now it's time to do something about it. But first, a caveat.

I can't tell you what to do. I don't know your business like you do. I experience risk differently than you. What I can tolerate is different than what you can tolerate. What I do for my business may not make sense for yours. I don't have the context to make one-size-fits-all prescriptions. Instead, what I will do is *describe* problems, questions to ask, ways you can approach risks, and what I did in my business. It's up to you to decide what's best for you.

First let's talk about timing. When is the best time to do something about risk? It's better to find out somebody is a vindictive psychopath *before* going into business with them. It's better to find out how much of a shitshow brick-and-mortar build-outs are *before* you begin. In your personal life, you'd rather find out if an area floods *before* you buy a house there. You get the idea. When it comes to risk, it's better to solve a cheap problem now than an expensive problem later. Now is always the best time to do something about risk.

Now let's look at valuing decisions. Decisions are investments of money, time, and energy. Good decisions are like good investments that give us more than we put in. Bad decisions are the opposite. Visiting my abuela at her old folks' home taught me a new way to value decisions. My abuela is a sweet old Cuban Humpty Dumpty. Decades of neglecting physical fitness left her too weak to support herself, so she kept falling and hurting herself. During this visit, she was in terrible pain, bedridden after yet another fall. Nurses had to use a machine to lift her from her bed to a wheelchair so she could use the bathroom.

Fuck. That.

Before, I thought of health and fitness as a way to look better and lift heavier stuff. That's part of it, of course. I wanted a nicer butt as much as the next person. But after seeing my abuela, I realized that wasn't even half the story. Being healthy was more about *not* winding up like her. Said another way, the benefits of being healthy were high, but the costs of *not* being healthy were higher. I sensed the same reasoning applied to everything. There was the benefit of doing something *and* the cost of not doing something. Looking at both together became the filter I use to value decisions.

Now let's look at another nuance: in what *order* do we make decisions? You're a busy person with busy-person stuff to do. You can't and shouldn't address all risks. That will drive you crazy and suck your energy from better things you could be doing. We have to be deliberate about where we put our time and energy. The first order of action is to look for low-hanging fruit: big risks with cheap solutions. In the real world this is like a seatbelt. Driving without one is dangerous, but taking a half second to buckle up is quick and easy and can save you in a crash. In investment terms, these are low-cost, high-return decisions.

One thing Brad regrets is not turning handshake agreements into written agreements. Hiring an attorney to draft up the agreements wouldn't have cost a lot and would have saved him a lot in the end. Other examples of low-hanging fruit could include outsourcing menial tasks, implementing basic cybersecurity protocols, or having simple conversations with your employees.

SCRAMBLING THE RISKABULARY

Now for the craziest part of this chapter: I'm going to change the vocabulary of risk. This may seem pedantic, but it will ultimately prove necessary and perhaps even revolutionary.

Why?

Businesses are complex networks of decisions. The quality of these decisions determines the quality of the business. Good decisions become good businesses. Bad decisions become dead businesses. The problem is that our current default vocabulary surrounding risk is useless at best and harmful at worst. So we're going to scrap it and replace it with a better vocabulary. Better words become better frames that become better decisions and better businesses. First let's look at some naughty words.

Reducing, Mitigating, and Eliminating Risk

All these words are variations on *less* risk. Sure, less risk is better than more risk, all else equal. Reducing, mitigating, and eliminating risk will be part of what we do, but it's not what we're optimizing for. Optimizing for less risk will suffocate your opportunities. It's like sacrificing the opportunity to make $10,000 so you can avoid losing $100. If you really want to optimize for less risk, the best thing you can do is have no business. That's not what we're here for. Risk is always a part of business, no matter how much you try to bubble-wrap it from disaster.

Taking and Managing Risk

I don't like the phrase "taking risk." It's not a bad frame, but its overuse has stripped it of all meaning. I don't like "managing risk" either. The word *managing* implies an active process in the same way managing a restaurant does. In reality, risk isn't so much the active consequence of management but the passive consequence of *design*.

Our Risk Frame: Choosing Risk

Think of your business like a house. With a house, some risks are actively managed. You clean and do routine maintenance so the house doesn't deteriorate. But there aren't any "managers" actively preventing houses from falling down. Houses stand because they are *designed* to stand.

Design is a network of choices. For a house to stand, engineers, architects, and builders have to choose the right blueprint, foundation, materials, and construction process. All decisions have different risks and opportunities. Some decisions mean cheaper construction costs but result in a poorer-quality house that needs constant maintenance. Other decisions might mean higher up-front costs but less maintenance and fewer headaches down the road. If people make the right choices, the house will last a long time. If they don't, it will fall apart.

Said another way, tomorrow's problems are consequences of yesterday's decisions.

Your business is also designed through a network of choices. You choose your industry, what you sell, where you operate, how you sell, and who you sell to. You choose the people you hire, fire, and partner with. You choose the tools you use and the agreements you commit to. You choose what to delegate, automate, and take on yourself. You choose how you make and spend money. Your risks and opportunities are consequences of these decisions. Choose well, and you will do well. Choose wrong, and you won't make it far.

Brad's problems with Float Temple were consequences of choices he made early on. Brad chose to open a brick-and-mortar float tank business. Brad chose his business partners. "I partnered with a business guy who didn't want to be in business, and another who was a vindictive psychopath," he said later on. Brad chose to rely on flimsy handshake agreements. Brad owns his choices: "I was a mediocre CEO. I made plenty of bad choices."

Of course, Brad benefited from his good choices too. Brad chose to build a business around something he loved and chose to build a great community.

What about your business? Are you in an easy or hard industry? Do you have business partners or employees? Do you sell digital or physical products? Do you sell to clients, customers, or sponsors? How have decisions like these shaped the risks and opportunities you face today?

THE RISK DESIGN PROTOCOLS

Now on to the **risk design protocols**. These are different ways you can design or redesign your business through networks of choices so that you can create better sets of risks and opportunities for yourself. Treat these protocols as options, not mandates. Some protocols will make more sense for your business than others. Do what makes sense given your circumstances. Focus on easy stuff first, and move to harder stuff later.

Simplify

Once you get fancy, fancy gets broken.
—Morgan Spurlock, filmmaker

Pessimists love bringing up Murphy's law: what can go wrong will go wrong. If that is true, so is the inverse. What can't go wrong won't go wrong (if nobody has claimed this idea, I'm calling it **Alexander's law**). That's why the most elegant and effective design protocol is to **simplify**. Simplification reduces the number of ways something can go wrong. Before you think of anything else, first think about how you can simplify. For example, Brad could have simplified Float Temple by attempting a less bureaucratically prone build-out process or by working with fewer business partners.

Diversify

You already know what **diversify** means: don't put all your eggs in one basket. It isn't just for stocks. Diversification spreads risks by increasing the number of things that have to go wrong for you to be affected. Putting eggs in multiple baskets means more baskets have to fall for you to run out of eggs. Diversification could mean marketing on multiple channels, opening a store in a different neighborhood, selling different types of products, working with multiple suppliers, or hiring multiple employees.

At Float Temple, Brad diversified by offering infrared sauna sessions, body-scanning services, and specialized coaching.

Have Backups

Two is one. One is none.
—Jocko Willink, scary Navy SEAL commander dude

Having a **backup** is as straightforward as it sounds. It's the spare tire, the backup freezer, the extra key to your house. In business, it can be the second employee who knows how to manage invoices, an extra freelancer, a backup piece of technology, a backup market to sell to, or extra money in the bank. Float Temple had three float chambers instead of one, so they always had some operational in case one wasn't working.

Backups could even be contingency plans. If that happens, I'll do this. If that employee leaves, I'll hand off their work to those other employees and activate my job postings. If Instagram shuts my account down, I'll double down on my YouTube channel. If this product stops selling well, I'll sell more of that. If I have to step away from the business, I'll put that person in charge. So on and so forth.

The Happy Hour Pivot

Broadly speaking, pivoting means changing how you do business. People talk about it all the time, but usually with big businesses. Everyone has heard the stories of companies like Facebook pivoting to mobile, the podcasting company that pivoted into Twitter, and Netflix pivoting from DVD rentals to streaming.

Nobody talks about small pivots. Businesses pivot every day without anybody realizing it. For example, imagine a steakhouse in Manhattan. Normally they sell hundred-dollar bottles of wine and hundred-dollar steaks to wealthy bankers and their wives/escorts. During Happy Hour, they shift to selling twenty-dollar cheeseburgers and half-priced cocktails—typically to entry-level employees at those same firms. The steakhouse pivots by selling different things to different people at different prices. *Pivoting changes the steakhouse's risk profile.* Wealthy bankers and their entry-level employees are *different* markets with *different* risks. Steaks and burgers are different products with different risks.

The beauty of the **Happy Hour pivot** is how easy it is. The steakhouse doesn't need a new kitchen, employees, or vendors. They only need to make a few small changes.

Happy Hour isn't their only pivot option. They can pivot by hosting private events, wedding parties, offering off-site catering, brunch, and to-go options. This is how a lot of restaurants survived the pandemic. When they couldn't host people inside, they shifted strategies and sold different things to different people in different ways—different products for different markets with different risks.

Efficiency versus Resilience

If you wanted a maximally fuel-efficient car, you would want the lightest car possible. Less weight means more miles per gallon. Simple enough. In order to do that, you would remove anything that added extra weight, which would include things like airbags, seatbelts, brake assist, and spare tires.

Of course, this would be ridiculous. Sure, you might eke out a few extra miles per gallon, but you would screw yourself over in a crash. This describes the tension between efficiency and resilience. Efficiency is great. Who doesn't want more output with less input? However, optimizing for efficiency eventually leads to making decisions that make you more vulnerable.

Remember that your first job as an entrepreneur isn't to be as efficient or make as much money as possible. Your first job is to survive. Expect to make decisions that increase costs or slow you down so that you can be more resilient. That's okay. It's better to be inefficiently alive than efficiently dead.

Throughout the rest of the book, we're going to dive deep into specific ways you can design or redesign your business. But to get a head start, begin thinking about changes you can make. How can you simplify your business? How can you diversify? How can you implement backups? What small Happy Hour pivots can you make?

KEY TAKEAWAYS

· Words matter. Good words create good frames and result in better outcomes.

· Value decisions by considering both the benefits and the costs of not making a decision.

· Focus on big risks before addressing small risks.

· Now is always the best time to do something about risks and opportunities.

· You can never totally eliminate risk in your business.

· Risk and opportunities are designed through networks of choices. How you design your business will determine your outcomes.

· Apply the risk design protocols to decide how you can simplify,
diversify, add backups, and pivot.

THE RISK RENAISSANCE CONCLUSION

What we have now, in metaphorical terms, is a metal detector and a shovel. We know how to detect risks and opportunities and what to do about them. The rest of this book is a road map of how to apply these lessons to your business. Each chapter has the same format: I will describe a risk, how to think about it, things you can do about it, and what I did about it in my business. This will help you do the same with yours.

The remaining chapters are ordered deliberately from big-picture external risks to the little-picture internal risks. Reading them in the order presented makes sense but isn't necessary. The foundation we've built will let you read any chapter in any order as your curiosity sees fit.

PART 2: EXTERNAL RISK

We live in an environment we don't control. We don't control the weather, temperature, mountains, rivers, oceans, wildlife, or natural disasters. Yet it's still our responsibility to survive. Environments can be harsh like Siberia or easy like sunny San Diego. The same goes for business. Business environments can be rife with opportunity or barren, opportunity-deprived deserts.

Everyone is a genius when times are good. Costs are low, supply chains are working smoothly, demand is high, laws are favorable, and interest rates are low. We're making more money than we know what to do with. The problem is when we assume good times will always be good. Our sunny San Diego–like environment can become a barren Siberian wasteland.

Everyone is a victim when times are bad. Costs rise, supply chains buckle, demand drops, interest rates rise, and laws become stricter. Money isn't easy anymore. We have a few choices when these things happen. We can do nothing and hope things get better. Or if we actually want to survive, we can take a hint from Canadians. Every winter, Canadians can choose to hunker down, play ice hockey, and eat poutine. Or they can go to Florida.

The lesson is that we don't control the environment, but we do control how we adapt and which environments we choose. This is why the first step to surviving our environment is understanding it. That means knowing what makes it habitable and why it would become uninhabitable. Next is understanding how we can adapt to our environment or change to a better one.

In Part 2: External Risk, we'll first look at your **industry**—things that don't change. Then we'll look at things that do: **markets**, **economics**, and **politics**.

CHAPTER 6

INDUSTRY RISK

"It's not a fucking brewpub," Rudy Delgado said, exasperated. "Look, here are the laws, the plans, and the exemptions, all *clearly* proving we are a *brewery* and not a brewpub." The distinction is important. Rudy has plans and permits for a brewery, not a brewpub. He has to convince the local zoning official of this. Otherwise, he won't be able to move forward with his plans.

"I feel like it's a brewpub, so it's a brewpub," the zoning official basically responded in a quick email.

"He completely ignored everything we sent! This isn't a feelings thing. This fucking guy has us by the balls, and he doesn't give a shit about doing his job. Now we have to get lawyers involved," Rudy fumed. This is one of the many headaches and hurdles Rudy had to clear to bring his dream, Rocketeer Brewery, to life.

Rudy is no stranger to projects. He's obsessed over model aircrafts, computers, car modifications, 3D printing, and tiki cocktails. He once spent forty hours putting together a 6,000-piece Lego Millennium Falcon. But nothing has fermented his excitement more than beermaking. "Beer is the intersection of craft, history, and science. I'm studying beers from sixteenth-century Germany and ancient Norway and playing with genetically modified hops. It's so much fun," Rudy explained.

Rudy is an excellent brewer. He's won awards for stouts, IPAs, and even an orange creamsicle sour. Pilsners are his favorite. "Everything has to be perfect. There's no room for error," Rudy said.

Rudy dreamed about owning his own brewery and eventually found the right partners to make it happen. It's far and away the most daunting thing he's ever tackled. It's his first business, and he's entering an industry with archaic laws, expensive machinery, webs of government bureaucracy, antagonistic corporate monopolies, and high investment costs. On top of this, he's raising two kids and working his nine-to-five corporate job.

Rudy feels the stress, but he is motivated. The brewery means a lot more than money and getting to play with beer. "Rocketeer Brewery can be a community center where people bring their families and make real connections. I want to sponsor baseball teams and give the neighborhood I've lived in for almost forty years the place it deserves. This can be the legacy I pass down to my kids or whoever wants to keep it alive."

Rudy also senses the cost of not opening his brewery. "I can't imagine waking up when I'm sixty doing the same menial corporate job. I can't go to my grave knowing I could have given it a shot but didn't."

Rudy methodically obsesses over every step of the process. Beer industry events have been his greatest source of knowledge. He's spent years geeking out with experienced brewery owners and asking them the same question: what do you wish you'd done differently?

The answers have been worth gold. "A lot of traumatized brewers straight-up tell me, 'Don't do it,'" Rudy noted. "I hear variations of this same story all the time."

"Watch out for distributors," brewers kept telling him. One brewer's story stood out: "I got seduced by a big offer and signed up with one of the nation's top distributors, but I didn't understand what I was getting myself into. Now I'm basically an indentured servant to a corporate monopoly."

Others have warned him about complicated taxes, ridiculous zoning issues, losing key employees, and buying the wrong equipment. He's also found really cool stuff he never would have found otherwise. "I didn't know there was so much software for us brewers. There are so many tools to track, measure, and manage every single step of the brewing process. It's amazing. Perfect for a tech nerd like me," Rudy says.

Rudy is still stressed, but the more he learns about what awaits him, the more relief he feels. "I'm so glad I'm finding these things out now. I can't imagine dealing with these problems when I'm paying rent." As of this writing, Rudy is set to open Rocketeer Brewery in Miami, Florida, in the spring of 2024.

To start our industry risk analysis, we're going to bring back our handy-dandy RDEE formula.

Risk = Damage x Existence x Exposure

DAMAGE: WHAT'S AT STAKE?

Mountains, deserts, tropical islands, and jungles are different terrains with their own unique challenges. On mountains, you have to deal with the cold and elevation. In the desert, heat and sandstorms. On tropical islands, earthquakes and hurricanes. In jungles, wild animals and poisonous insects.

The risk is that you won't survive your terrain. You won't be able to handle the cold of the mountains, the storms of the islands, the heat of the desert, or the animals of the jungle.

In business, your industry is your terrain. All industries have a unique and default set of risks you'll encounter just by being in the industry. The risk is that you'll wind up like many who came before you: unable to handle the challenges your industry throws at you.

EXISTENCE: WHAT RISKS EXIST?

Industry risks are the unavoidable risks you inherit by being in your industry—the risks all businesses like yours deal with.

Brewery owners all have to deal with complex machines, tricky laws, and making beer that, at the very least, tastes decent and doesn't poison their customers. There exists a chance a brewery owner gets tangled in messy legal problems, equipment breaks, and failed quality controls. The same logic applies for all industries.

Car mechanic shops have to deal with finding and retaining competent mechanics, managing clients, making sure their machinery works, and the supply chains for repair parts. Law firms have to deal with Bar Association rules and regulations, chasing down clients for money, and the complexities of judicial bureaucracies. Restaurants have to maintain cleanliness for food inspectors, source ingredients, repair kitchen equipment, and not poison their customers.

That's the key. Shared risks are predictable risks. If you see businesses like yours run into certain problems, you're probably going to run into those problems yourself. Once you know what to look out for, you can take measures to avoid them.

Describe one major problem all businesses in your industry have.

Now let's zoom in further and look at nonobvious industry risks you may inherit.

Direct

Direct risks are the risks all businesses in your industry deal with. Breweries have to deal with the same risks other breweries deal with, restaurants with other restaurants, law firms with other law firms, hair salons with other hair salons, etc.

Hybrid

Some businesses are hybrid-industry businesses. Take a business doing international plant medicine retreats. They have to deal with travel logistics, the politics of host countries, and currency fluctuations, along with the occasional existential meltdowns of their clients. A restaurant doubling as a wedding venue will have to deal with food safety, ingredient sourcing, kitchen management, along with out-of-control groomsmen and psychotic brides.

Indirect

A business can also adopt another industry's risks. Recall the Detroit barber from the "transfer risk" section. The barber directly inherits barber industry risks. However, given that his clients all work in the auto industry, he also adopts auto industry risks. Take a marketing agency that makes TV commercials for hotel chains. The agency directly inherits marketing agency risks and indirectly inherits hotel industry risks.

If any apply, describe a hybrid or indirect industry risk you face.

EXPOSURE: HOW VULNERABLE ARE YOU?

Let's look at your exposure to industry risks in two ways: the industry itself and the kind of person you are.

The Lindy Effect

If you're going to build something, you should know how stable the foundation is. All industries are different, but there's a simple test to determine how much that foundation will change.

Nassim Taleb describes the **Lindy effect** in his book *Antifragile*. It's also known as the reverse aging principle. The logic goes that the older something is, the longer it will go on living. This explains anything "classic" from architecture styles, music, movies, restaurants, to books. Plato, the Bible, Roman Corinthian columns, Shakespeare, Beethoven, and *The Godfather* (parts 1 and 2) aren't disappearing anytime soon. The same goes for industries.

Classic industries are less likely to change or disappear. These include real estate, entertainment, farming, clothing, funeral services, alcohol, and weapons manufacturing. Those industries will go away when people stop needing places to live, be entertained, wear clothes, die, get drunk, and fight each other. In other words, never. Rudy from Rocketeer Brewery is entering an ancient industry: alcohol. It's unlikely he'll have problems here.

Newer industries are less stable. Their roles haven't been rooted in civilization for long. They're more likely to change or disappear entirely. This explains the fate of short-lived phenomena like VCRs, cassette tapes, most cryptocurrencies, fad diets, and overly hyped technology companies. The less time it's been around, the less time it will likely survive.

What about your industry? How long has yours been around?

Kiddie Poolers and Pacific Oceaners

How prepared you are for your industry depends on your personality. Imagine two people learning to swim. One learns by jumping into the Pacific Ocean. The other watches YouTube swim tutorials before dipping their toes in a kiddie pool.

Rudy is a cautious **Kiddie Pooler** who spent eight years as an amateur home brewer before jumping into professional brewing. To avoid learning things the hard way, he is meticulously studying and preemptively resolving the traps that could surprise him once his brewery is open.

Pacific Oceaners bravely/recklessly jump into the unknown with little preparation. This includes people like Brad Larsen from Float Temple, who is the kind of person who decides to do something first and figures out how later. They are more likely to find their industry's traps the hard way.

Neither is inherently better than the other. Some Kiddie Poolers will learn to avoid predictable traps and thrive, while others will overanalyze and never get in the water. Some Pacific Oceaners will figure it out and thrive, while others will get eaten by sharks. All businesses require venturing into the unknown. How you venture into the unknown will clue you in to which problems you're most likely to have. Know your tendencies. Know your risks.

Take a moment to reflect on which type you are. In your life, have you been more a meticulous planner or a figure-things-out-on-the-go type?

INDUSTRY OPPORTUNITIES

You won't be the first person to succeed in your industry. Others have been where you are right now and have become successful. Connect to their stories, and discover potential new upsides you might not have seen otherwise that can give you clues about how to find your own. Dig into more than the money you can make. What are other potential upsides? What kinds of people could you meet along the way? What fun, exciting work could you do? What lifestyle changes are possible along this path? Connecting to new upsides will give you more energy to do the work needed to get there.

At Rocketeer Brewery, Rudy is excited about the money he can make if things go well, but he sees a lot more than that. He sees an opportunity to escape his bland nine-to-five corporate life and instead spend his days perfecting new beers with his best friend and business partner. He sees an opportunity to build a vibrant community center where he can foster deeper relationships with his neighbors. Although he's hesitant to dream past the current scope of Rocketeer's opening, he can't help but imagine a greater constellation of exciting food-and-drink-related businesses. Beyond even that, Rudy sees a chance to create a legacy that he can pass down to his family. Sensing these opportunities makes it a lot easier for him to deal with incompetent government zoning officials.

CHOOSING INDUSTRY RISKS

Most industries have communities, conferences, books, and podcasts where people gather and discuss their triumphs and misfortunes. Study their stories so you can discover common traps and surprising opportunities.

Name one place—physical or online—where you can learn from others in your industry.

This is Rudy's strategy. He attends beer industry events to learn from veteran brewers. By asking, "What did you wish you'd done differently?" Rudy is better able to build a map of the traps that lie ahead. Along the way, Rudy has also encountered opportunities in the form of time-saving management technology he wouldn't have known about otherwise. All of this means Rudy is reducing the odds he falls into predictable traps and increasing the odds he finds profitable new opportunities.

When it comes to external risks, you can't change the environment, but you can switch environments. You probably won't change your industry, but you can change the industries you work with. Take a hotel marketing agency. The agency will always have marketing agency risks, but it doesn't have to have hotel industry risks. The agency can change its industry risks by changing the industries it works with. For example, they can switch from working with hotel industry clients to accounting industry clients. Different industries. Different risks.

The better you get at understanding an industry's risks and opportunities, the better you will be at choosing those that best suit you.

Describe one way you can change your industry risks.

TACO STREET AND INDUSTRY RISK

Real estate is a classic industry. People always need somewhere to live. That's not going away anytime soon.

A commission-based business like apartment locating is interesting because much of the money I make has nothing to do with how hard I work. I can spend months with a client without making a dime and a few hours with another and make $5,000. This makes the industry scary and exciting. If I do it right, I can build a strong connection to a stable industry and create a reliable income source.

In the beginning I was a Kiddie Pooler. Before Taco Street, I worked at a local apartment locating agency I'll call Cool Apartment Agency. I saw a few people making tens of thousands of dollars each month, but most were barely getting by. I had to learn why. It was the difference between staying broke and earning six figures and traveling whenever I wanted.

These were the common traps I saw.

Lead flow: People who relied on company leads rather than learning how to get their own all quit. They couldn't close enough deals to survive.

Failing to stand out: Everyone presented themselves the same way. Nobody stood out. Their clients kept ghosting them.

Delayed payments: Locators get paid months after transactions close. Many dropped out because they couldn't handle the inconsistent and delayed cash flow.

Overwhelm and burnout: Working with one client is easy. Working with many is not. I saw many locators burn out because they couldn't handle their sales pipeline.

The successful ones were great lead generators, offered a good service, and were organized. A part of me felt I was smarter than they were, so I got the confidence that I could do better.

So I did. I learned how to get my own leads so I was always busy closing deals. I designed a better service so clients would want to work with me. Being dead-broke and splitting rent with my best friend meant I was already living cheap. I could handle the delayed cash flow better than somebody with a mortgage and car payment.

I built strong operations. Where my colleagues were using pen and paper and messy spreadsheets, I was using professional sales software and hiring freelancers. That meant closing more deals while spending less of my own energy.

KEY TAKEAWAYS

· Your industry has a unique set of risks and opportunities. Learn from others to discover what they are.

· Pay attention to industries whose risks you adopt directly or indirectly.

· Know if you're in a classic and stable industry or a modern and unstable one.

· Know if you're the kind of person who will cautiously or recklessly jump into the unknown.

· Research, but accept that nothing replaces experience. Watching YouTube swimming tutorials never beats actual swimming.

CHAPTER 7

MARKET RISK

There was an old, abandoned gas station in East Austin. The city was growing fast. This former bad part of town was becoming the cool part of town. A local family saw the writing on the wall, took over the space, and turned it into Lazarus Brewing.

Fast-forward a few years, and they've since become one of the most popular spots in the neighborhood. The beer is great. The tacos are tasty. The vibes are strong. They're always busy. Everything is great, right?

Not exactly.

The more money they made, the more money they paid the landlord. The landlord had leverage. He owned the space. The market was booming, and real estate prices were soaring. If it came to it, he could probably find another tenant who would pay more than the brewery. This put Lazarus's owners in a conundrum. Despite surface success, they were at risk of the rental market pricing them out of business.

So the owners did something clever. They opened up a second location. But this time, instead of renting the new space, they *bought* it. Buying their new space meant the rising rental market wouldn't put them out of business.

Risk = Damage x Existence x Exposure

DAMAGE: WHAT'S AT STAKE?

Humans need habitable climates. We would die if summers reached 200 degrees or winters dropped to negative 100. Similarly, businesses need habitable climates to survive.

In simplified terms, where real-world climate is the balance between hot and cold, business climate is the relationship between supply and demand. All businesses use stuff to make stuff (supply) and sell it (demand). A market is the relationship between supply and demand. You need both for a habitable market to exist.

Selling sand in the desert: supply; no demand. No market. No business.
Selling snow in the desert: demand; no supply. No market. No business.
Selling water in the desert: supply; demand. Market. You're in business!

For better and worse, you are at the mercy of markets outside your control. **Market risk** is whatever makes your business climate less habitable. This means whatever makes business more expensive to run and/or money harder to make.

Market risk is about the following questions:
• What are your markets?
• What conditions do you need to survive?
• Why do markets shift?
• How would a shift impact you?
• What can you do about it?

EXISTENCE: WHAT RISKS EXIST?

You need supply to make stuff and demand to sell stuff. Let's look at both sides.

Supply is whatever you use to run your business. Supply markets could be interest rates for loans, labor for employees, rent for space, ingredients for food, materials, advertising costs, or software licensing fees.

Demand is whoever pays you, such as clients, customers, and sponsors. Demand markets come in many forms: demographic (young adults aged eighteen to twenty-five), psychographic (Japanese anime fans), geographic (people in East Austin), or a blend (young adult anime fans living in East Austin). They can also be other businesses (hospitals, software companies, etc.).

Knowing your market risks means knowing your markets and how they behave. Let's say you're the proud owner of a cool, hip brewery in East Austin.

On the supply side, you need hops and grains for raw ingredients, fancy beermaking machines, employees to make beer, and space to operate in. Each is a different market: the hops market, grain market, labor market, fancy beer machine market, and commercial real estate market. You won't survive if these markets become too expensive to make a profit.

On the demand side, you sell beer two ways: inside your taproom to East Austin locals and through local stores that sell cans of your beer. These are two markets: neighborhood locals and the stores that sell your beer. You can't survive if you don't make enough money from locals coming to your taproom or if stores don't sell enough of your beer.

For each supply-and-demand side market, there exists a chance it could turn against you.

Take a minute to describe your markets. List the inputs you need to create what you sell (supply), and describe the people who pay you (demand).

EXPOSURE: HOW VULNERABLE ARE YOUR MARKETS?
You can't predict markets, but knowing how they work is a good start.

Let's look at how the brewery's markets might change. A natural disaster or rising fertilizer prices could drive up hop and grain prices. New breweries could open, offer higher salaries, and drive up labor costs. The supply chain for beer equipment could slow down, making it harder to come by. New businesses opening could drive up commercial real estate prices.

On the demand side, a major employer could shut down, causing people to start moving away. Crime could spike in the neighborhood, and people wouldn't want to go to your brewery anymore. Other brewers could offer more money to shop owners to sell their beer. Your customers could buy less beer because of health reasons.

Expense Concentration (Supply) and Relative Market Size (Demand)

How sensitive are you to market shifts? Let's look at this question two ways.

The greater the expense, the greater the impact. For example, if 10 percent of your costs are hops and grains and 60 percent of your costs come from rent, you are more sensitive to a 10 percent jump in rent costs than you are to a 10 percent jump in the cost of hops and grains.

Now for the demand side. Your sensitivity depends on your size relative to your market. It's the year 2000. Five thousand people live in East Austin. Here your brewery is a **big slice** of the market. A major employer leaves town, and 1,000 people leave the neighborhood—a 20 percent decline. This is a big shock.

It's the year 2022. Twenty thousand people live in East Austin. Now you're a **small slice** of the market. The same employer leaves, and 1,000 people leave the neighborhood. This time it's only a 5 percent decline—a smaller shock.

Obviously, the 20 percent decline would be more dramatic than the 5 percent decline. Big-slice businesses are more sensitive to market shifts than small-slice businesses.

What about you? Do you have any hyperconcentrated expenses? Is yours a big-slice or a small-slice business?

MARKET OPPORTUNITIES

Market shifts go both ways. Good shifts happen for the same reasons bad ones do. Prices for inputs like rent and ingredients can fall. New residential buildings can open up in the neighborhood and spike local demand. New markets, like the sparkling water or hard seltzer markets, can appear out of nowhere and open up new diversified revenue sources. Different markets have different risks and opportunities. Every market you can access but aren't is an opportunity to improve your risk profile and/or make more money. You may discover better markets with better prices and higher demand.

Treat your size as an advantage. You don't have the same resources a big business does, but they don't have the same agility or human touch you do. It's why small local breweries can make fun taprooms and exciting craft beers, while big conglomerates only make glorified piss-water.

CHOOSING MARKET RISK

You don't control markets. But you do choose them. Knowing how to choose the right markets is how you'll survive bad shifts and take advantage of good ones.

Back to your hypothetical brewery. From the supply side, let's look at the two major expenses: ingredients and rent.

Supply Side

You're worried about rising hop and grain prices squeezing beer profits. You can use your existing equipment and shift to making alcoholic kombucha, which doesn't use hops or grains. This would mean hop and grain price spikes wouldn't affect you as much.

You're worried rental prices will spike more than you can handle. You can eliminate rental market risk by exiting the market altogether. That's what the owners of Lazarus Brewing did when they bought their second space. More accurately, buying real estate meant trading rental market risks for business loan and commercial real estate market risks.

Demand Side

On the demand side, let's look at where your sales come from: neighbors and local beer shops. You notice your customers are becoming more carb-conscious, drinking less beer, and quitting drinking all together. You can use your existing equipment to make sparkling water, no-carb hard seltzer, and boozy kombucha, and you can invite food trucks to sell tacos.

You can also sell your beer to stores in other cities and spread your risk across multiple markets.

Reality Check: Just because you can shift markets doesn't mean you should. What you don't want to do is shift into a worse market or make things more complicated than they're worth. Treat pivot markets as options. Look at them the same way you would existing ones.

Describe one simple way you can change your market risks.

TACO STREET AND MARKET RISK

We make money from apartment complexes paying us commissions when our clients move into their buildings. How much they pay us depends on the market. In good markets, they pay us a lot. In bad markets, they pay little or nothing at all.

Our market has apartment buildings on the supply side and people looking for them on the demand side. If there aren't enough apartments, people won't have many options. Apartments can sit back waiting for people to come and slash commissions. That's why our business model doesn't work in places like New York and San Francisco where the demand is much higher than the supply.

On the demand side, if there aren't enough people looking for apartments, we don't have clients. It wouldn't matter if there were a million apartments paying giant commissions.

The best climate is when there are lots of people looking for apartments and lots of apartments for them to choose from. That's been the case for most of my time with Taco Street. We've had plenty of clients to work with and plenty of apartments that pay us high commissions. It's why 2020, the pandemic year, was our best year ever. People were flocking to Austin, and apartments were paying high commissions. This means a lot of my success with Taco Street has nothing to do with me but with market forces outside my control.

Early in 2022, Austin's market turned against us. Too many people were moving here, and there weren't enough apartments for them to choose from. Apartments lowered commissions or stopped paying them altogether. My once-fertile market was becoming too hot. Luckily, at least for me, the recession that began later that year cooled the market down back to a better supply-demand balance.

I knew this market problem had been an issue years before. I didn't like the risk of relying on a single market to survive. It's why I Happy Hour pivoted Taco Street into Houston and Dallas. It was easy. All it took was some minor adjustments. Both were rife with opportunity, but more importantly, I spread my risk from one market to three. When Austin's market was worsening, I started doing more business in Dallas and Houston.

Pivoting also changed our relative size to the market. We went from a small business in a medium market to a small business in a massive combined market. We only need a small slice of a huge market to survive. Even if aliens blasted Austin off the face of the earth, I could just shift to Dallas or Houston and be fine.

On the supply side, anything that could restrict apartment supply is a risk. Politics could get in the way (more on this later). Something I didn't take into consideration was construction costs. In 2022, lumber prices skyrocketed. If apartments became too expensive to build, that would be a real longer-term problem. The price spike didn't last long, but it did freak me out.

Overall, I'm comfortable with Taco Street's market risk. Being a small-slice business in three large markets with high supply and demand means we should always have a market to work with.

KEY TAKEAWAYS

- Businesses, like people, need habitable climates. Understand your climate by understanding your markets and the conditions that make your business possible.

- Look at the input (supply) and output (demand) sides of your market. Think about how those conditions might change, how you'd be affected, and how you can adapt.

- The better you understand your market, the better you can take advantage of good shifts and defend against bad ones.

CHAPTER 8

ECONOMIC RISK

Scribe Media sells professional book services that include ghostwriting, coaching, editing, publishing, and marketing. From its founding, Scribe grew like wildfire. Revenue and team size were multiplying every year. Everything went haywire when the pandemic broke out. Scribe had a big problem. Theirs was a *luxury* service. It was the kind of service that flourished in good times and floundered in bad times. People aren't as aggressive on marketing when they're worried about rent or taxes.

Scribe was fucked. Overnight their sales calendar dried up. Incoming revenues froze. They went from an exploding success story to one that could be dead in weeks. Rather than sit back and "hope things got better," they took action. They launched a free webinar where people could learn how to write their own books.

Based on feedback, Scribe built a *cheaper modified* version of their flagship service called the Coached Author Program. I was one of their first new customers. Many people bought this program, which generated enough revenue for Scribe to make it through the first critical months of the pandemic.

For Scribe, the pandemic had upsides. Remote work meant people were still making money, and lockdowns meant people had more time to write their books.

When the world changed, Scribe changed. This last-minute Happy Hour pivot helped them adapt to a new environment. (Unfortunately, this is not where Scribe's story ends. I'll revisit their story later in the book.)

Risk = Damage x Existence x Exposure

DAMAGE: WHAT'S AT STAKE?

All climates have natural disasters: droughts, hurricanes, snowstorms, earthquakes, fires, etc. Business climates have natural disasters too—economic ones. Crashes, depressions, recessions, or whatever you want to call them have been happening for as long as economies have existed. Yet time and time again, people get caught off guard as if it's the first time it's ever happened.

Crises aren't common, but they are inevitable. As of this writing, the last major economic crisis was in 2008. You probably didn't start your business until after that, so you don't know what it's like to go through one. That means you're probably not prepared. So how do you prepare for something that is both potentially devastating and inevitable?

To understand how a crash might affect you, you have to understand how economics works. Given that I have a fancy undergraduate degree in economics from a prestigious university, I'm more than qualified to explain it. People trade stuff. The more people trade, the more money they make. The less people trade, the less money they make. In a crash, people trade less and make less money. There you go. That's economics.

But you're not here to learn economics, why crashes happen, or how everyone will be impacted. You're interested in how you can survive a crash. At its core, an economic crash is a dramatic market shift. They happen for different reasons, affect different industries in different ways, and vary in length and severity. The wrong crisis at the wrong time can make your environment uninhabitable.

Let's look at what you sell and who you sell it to, but this time through the lens of an economic crisis.

EXISTENCE: WILL A CRASH HAPPEN?

If there is an economy, there exists a chance it will crash. And it's not if. It's when and how. **Economic risk** centers around one question: what happens when the people you rely on to have money have less of it?

EXPOSURE: HOW VULNERABLE ARE YOU TO A CRASH?

That depends on what you sell and who you sell it to. Let's look at both sides.

Is Your Product a Necessity or a Luxury?

Whatever you sell falls on a spectrum between something people need (**necessity**) and something people don't need (**luxury**). People cut their bottle-service-at-clubs budget before they cut their toilet-paper-and-rent budget. Companies cut their Christmas party and marketing budgets before cutting their accounting department. The more luxurious your product, the more vulnerable it is.

What Percent of Your Customers' Income Is the Price of Your Product?

Budget load is the percent of somebody's income they spend on your product. The bigger the budget load, the more sensitive it is. People cut high-budget stuff before they cut low-budget stuff. A $3,000 trip to Spain and a $75 bottle of tequila are both luxuries, but people will more likely cut the Spain trip before the tequila bottle.

Here's an oversimplified matrix.

Necessary + Low-Budget: everyday essentials like toilet paper, toothpaste, soap, and utilities. *Risk—super low.*

Necessary + High-Budget: rent, mortgage, taxes, groceries, healthcare, and accounting. *Risk—low to medium.*

Luxury + Low-Budget: hair and nail salons, fancy bottles of tequila, a Netflix subscription. *Risk—medium.*

Luxury + High-Budget: fancy cars, fancy trips to Europe, an experimental product launch, an extravagant Christmas party, flashy marketing campaigns, or a $10,000 life-coaching program. *Risk—super high!*

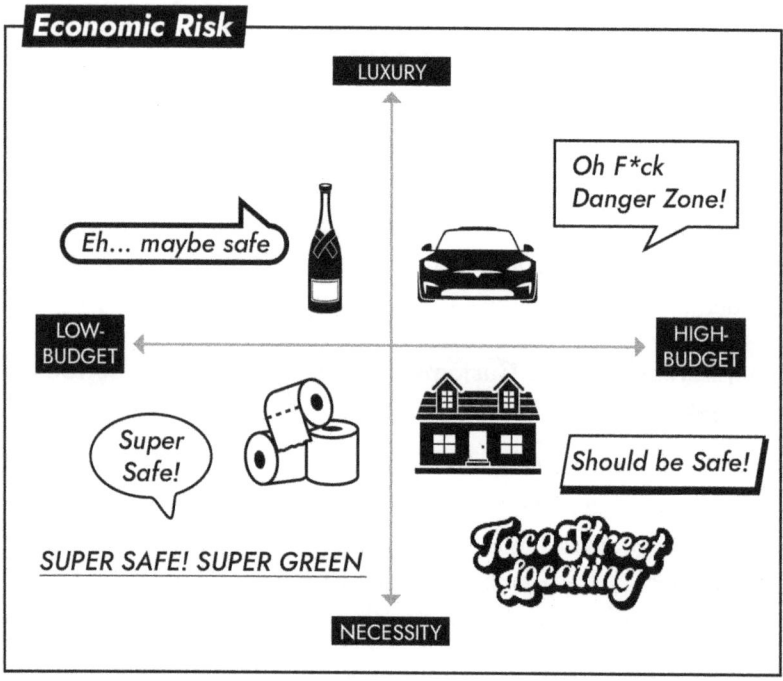

Take a moment to look at how your customers relate to your product or service. Is it a luxury or a necessity? Does your product make up a big or small portion of their budget?

Then there's your market. Their risks are your risks. You have a problem if the people who pay you can't pay you anymore. Look at your customers and clients. Wealthy people are less likely to go broke than poor ones. A yoga studio catering to tech executives is safer than one catering to teachers. Consultants for cash-tight startups and nonprofits are more vulnerable than consultants for profitable publicly traded corporations.

What industries are your customers in? Finance analysts have finance industry risks. Software engineers have tech industry risks. Nurses take on healthcare industry risks. Their risks become your risks.

A strip club in Manhattan, the China Club, found this out the hard way. They went bankrupt shortly after the investment bank Lehman Brothers—where most of their clients came from—went out of business. The more vulnerable your clients are, the more vulnerable you are.

Describe your customers. How sensitive are they to economic shocks? How would they behave if they suddenly had less money?

ECONOMIC OPPORTUNITIES

Good economies create obvious opportunities. Stuff is cheap, and demand is high. There's plenty of money to make.

The goal is to find opportunities in bad times. Imagine yourself, at least for a moment, as a vulture. Crashes will destroy many businesses around you. Terrible for them, but great for a hungry bird like you. Their laid-off employees can become your employees. Their clients and customers can become your customers. Their vacated retail spaces can become your retail space. So on and so forth.

Surviving bad times means you get to take advantage of good times. Don't think about downturns as recessions or crashes but shifts. People don't stop doing business. They do business in other ways. Different circumstances create different behaviors, which create different opportunities.

CHOOSING ECONOMIC RISK

Learn from past crashes. Your industry isn't new. Businesses like yours aren't new. Crashes aren't new. Study how businesses like yours do in downturns. How do people behave? Do people buy more or less of your products? What do they buy instead? You may find businesses like yours aren't affected much, or even do better in recessions.

You don't control the economy, but you do control what you sell and who you sell it to. Different products and different markets have different risks.

Product Shift: Can You Change What You Sell?

Can you sell a different version of your existing product? Maybe it's a cheaper version of your main service that more people can afford. This is what Scribe did.

Market Shift: Can You Change Who You Sell To?

Can you sell your existing service to a different market? For example, a marketing agency could pivot from working with boutique hotels to working with accounting firms.

Can You Change Both?

Can you offer a different version of your product to a different market? During the pandemic, a Southern restaurant in Austin named Olamaie pivoted from fancy dinners to biscuit sandwiches to go. It was a slightly different version of something the restaurant already sold lots of. The biscuits were so popular they spun that off into a new business: Little Ola's Biscuits.

TACO STREET AND ECONOMIC RISK

Real estate is notoriously sensitive to economic shifts. The 2008 financial crisis might as well have been the Black Death. Between 2006's peak and 2012's bottom, the number of real estate agents in the US shrunk by almost 30 percent.[1]

Fortunately, at Taco Street, we don't have the same risks. We don't buy or sell houses. We work with rental apartments. Like traditional agents, we make money on transactions. More transactions means more money.

Our business works in all economies. The main reason is that we work with a necessary product. People need places to live. People will cut almost everything else before they cut their rent budgets. When people can't afford down payments on houses, they rent apartments. When they can't afford their mortgages, they sell their houses and rent apartments. When they can't afford their apartments, they rent cheaper ones or get roommates. In good economies, companies hire more people who relocate to new cities and rent apartments.

On the other side, apartment buildings need people. Return-on-investment-maximizing investors own apartment buildings. They would rather pay high commissions to people like us than pay for empty units. In my experience, the more worried they are, the higher the commissions they pay out. This was why commissions rose during the pandemic and the mass tech layoffs in late 2022.

The only thing I can imagine going wrong is the economy getting so bad that apartments can't afford to pay commissions anymore. I don't think that will happen, but I can't rule it out.

Then there are our markets. Their risks are our risks. Whatever threatens the economies in Austin, Dallas, and Houston threatens us. If

---

1 National Association of Realtors, https://www.nar.realtor/membership/historic-report.

businesses stop hiring, we'll have fewer clients. Each city has many industries. Tech in Austin, oil and gas in Houston, and pretty much everything in Dallas. Their diversity is our diversity. In a crash, some industries will shrink and lay off employees. Others will thrive and hire more.

On a national scale, Texas cities are cheaper than other major US cities like New York and Los Angeles. When people have less money, they leave expensive cities for cheaper cities, which means more clients for us. I'm comfortable with our economic risk. We're not immune, but given our product and markets, we're positioned to do well in any economic situation.

KEY TAKEAWAYS

· What has happened before will happen again. Hoping things will get better will not save you.

· Understand your product's relationship to your customers and clients. Their risks become your risks. Study businesses and products like yours in past recessions for clues.

· Look for ways to change your product or service—or both. Do this well, and you will thrive in good times and survive in bad times. If you do it right, you can thrive no matter what.

CHAPTER 9

POLITICAL RISK

Airbnb came on the scene in 2008, and before long, a small niche industry exploded into a global phenomenon now known as the short-term rental industry. People everywhere began renting out everything from living room couches, spare rooms, suburban houses, yurts, campsites, villas, and anything anyone would pay to stay in. Ever since then, it's been a multidimensional political tug-of-war between entrepreneurs who want to make money, travelers who want cheaper and more interesting places to stay, locals who don't want to get priced out of their neighborhoods, and big corporate hotel chains seeking to eliminate competition.

Everyone who can make rules is putting their hands in the political cookie jar. Counties levy occupancy taxes. Neighborhoods impose zoning restrictions. Homeowner associations limit nightly rentals. Cities introduce permitting requirements. Combined, they force short-term rental homeowners to pretzel themselves in increasingly complex ways to avoid fines and lawsuits. Many exit the business altogether, but some get creative and change the rules that apply to them.

The short-term rental industry's young age poses a problem. Older industries have long-established rules that create predictability and stability. Rules in this newer industry are changing constantly as regulators try to figure out what to do. Anybody looking to make a living in the business has to deal with the fact that the rules may change at any time.

Risk = Damage x Existence x Exposure

DAMAGE: WHAT'S AT STAKE?

It's a simulation.

There. I said it.

Yeah, you kinda knew it all along. Things seemed a bit too fishy. People called you crazy, but you knew. I'm here to tell you you're not crazy. You were right all along. This "business environment" of yours is a simulation.

People everywhere at all times are monkeying around at the control panel of your environment. They include politicians, central bankers, government bureaucrats, eccentric billionaires, homeowners' associations, zoning commissions, licensing boards, and politically connected corporate executives. They tinker with interest rates, laws, taxes, decrees, restrictions, ordinances, regulations, and permitting requirements. Each change impacts your environment. Anyone who's been on the wrong side of complex bureaucratic red tape, powerful big-industry lobbying groups, forced lockdowns, and suffocating tax regimes has found this out the hard way.

With simple pen strokes, people can transform your business environment from a thriving ecosystem into a barren wasteland. Making things more complicated, these rule-tinkerers themselves change. Today's friendly rule-makers may become tomorrow's unfriendly rule-makers and vice versa.

In this chapter, we're going to look at **political risk:** how political forces can change your environment and what you can do about it. For this chapter, we'll presume you recently listened to Dan Carlin's long podcast series about Genghis Khan and the Mongolian Empire and are now the proud owner of a Mongolian yurt-themed short-term rental business. Congratulations!

EXISTENCE: WHAT RISKS EXIST?

There are two sets of rules: those that exist and can be changed and those that don't exist but could. The point isn't to identify everything but to isolate the few changes that would have the most impact. For the short-term rental industry, we'll isolate three rules commonly changed or introduced.

Permitting

Many cities require permits to operate short-term rentals. The risk is that you won't be able to obtain or retain the permission required to rent your lovely yurts short term. If you lose your permit, you either won't get to participate in the industry anymore, or you'll have to risk the fines of doing it illegally. Here you should be on the lookout for any rules that make permitting harder to acquire or retain.

Nightly Limits

A common rule allows cities and homeowner associations to impose limits on how long people can rent their homes for. For example, you may not rent your yurt for less than thirty days at a time. This rule effectively outlaws short-term rentals. Other rules restrict how many nights per year you are allowed to rent space for. For example, you might not be able to rent your yurt for more than ninety total nights of the year. If you were subject to these restrictions, you would have to shut down, work illegally, or find a workaround.

Occupancy Taxes

Some cities place additional taxes, known as occupancy taxes, on short-term rentals, which makes doing business more expensive.

EXPOSURE: HOW LIKELY WILL RULES CHANGE?

This depends on a few things.

Your Industry

Different industries fall on different points of the regulatory spectrum. Some are hyperregulated (healthcare, alcohol, oil and gas), while others are largely ignored (supplements, marketing).

Beware Transfer Risk: Your industry may be lightly regulated, but your client's industries may be heavily regulated. Their risks become your risks. The more regulatory your industry, the more likely additional regulations will happen.

Industry age is another factor. Newer industries like short-term rentals and cryptocurrencies may not have many regulations now, but you can expect more rules as their impact on society unfolds.

Your Markets

Places like California and New York tend to be more regulatory, while my glorious state of Texas tends to be more relaxed. This varies the more local you get. Counties, cities, and neighborhoods all have their own political microclimates. Your location lies somewhere on the California-to-Texas spectrum.

Beware Transfer Risk: You can adopt outside political risks too. Do you import stuff from China? Chinese political risks are now your political risks. Do you buy coffee beans from Colombia? Their risks are your risks.

Here's another oversimplified matrix.

California Regulations + High-Regulation Industry: *Risk—high.*

California Regulations + Low-Regulation Industry: *Risk—medium.*

Texas Regulations + High-Regulation Industry: *Risk—medium.*

Texas Regulations + Low-Regulation Industry: *Risk—wild west, no rules!*

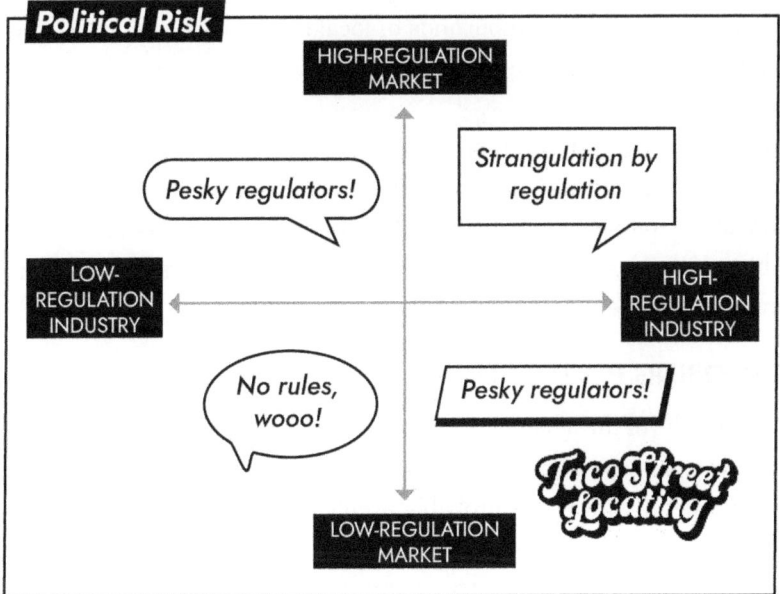

Like before, this matrix is a good place to start, but for a better picture, study similar businesses and markets to see what kind of regulations you can expect.

For example, say you rent out your yurts in a serene desert in New Mexico. You know short-term rentals are often highly regulated, but regulations in New Mexico are currently easy to deal with. However, there's been a lot of political noise around short-term rentals lately, and there's an election coming soon. You want to be on the lookout for how things may shake out. Look at more restrictive states for examples.

POLITICAL OPPORTUNITY

Rule changes can be good or bad. A new group of simulation-rule-tin-kerers can come in and make your environment easier. Lower taxes. Fewer regulations. Maybe some new loopholes open up.

Weed legalization across US states has opened the door for thousands of entrepreneurs all over the country. Similarly, when the US legalized homebrewing, it led to thousands of local breweries opening all over the country.

Even bad political shifts create opportunities. Those who don't survive leave space for those who do. Prohibition was a death sentence for honest businesspeople but a boon for organized crime mafias. Those who survive bad political environments will have an advantage if rules improve. Different rules, different opportunities.

CHOOSING POLITICAL RISK

For the sake of this chapter, I'm going to take a pessimistic stance and presume you won't change your political environment. Sure, you can vote (hopefully). But you probably aren't large enough to "campaign finance" yourself favorable rules, and you probably don't have enough time or energy to join industry groups, protests, and board meetings.

If you can, great. But we'll focus on what you can do inside your business by taking a similar approach to what we've done in the previous chapters. We've talked about how you don't control the environment, but you do control which environment you're in. Here you don't control the rules, but you do control which rules you're subject to based on the environment you're in.

Change Markets

Specific rules differ between locations, but the distinctions below are generally the same.

Short-term rentals are anything under thirty days. They're subject to occupancy taxes, local ordinances, homeowner associations, and licensing requirements. Each is a pain to navigate. Rentals *over* thirty days are considered medium-term rentals, which aren't subject to short-term rental laws. Medium-term rental laws are much easier to deal with than short-term rental laws. Short-term and medium-term rentals (say, one to six months) are different consumer markets too.

Short-term rentals cater to travelers, tourists, and drunk bachelor(ette) parties, while medium-term rentals might cater to traveling nurses, corporate consultants, and people renovating their homes. This is a Happy Hour pivot. Switching between short-term and medium-term markets only takes some minor adjustments.

Change Environments

You don't control the environment, but you do control which environment you operate in. A more drastic change for your short-term rental yurt business may be changing where you do business. You can embrace the nomadic spirit of your appropriated Mongolian ancestors and relocate your yurt business from a politically hostile area to a politically favorable one.

Different markets = different rules, different risks, different opportunities.

Change Products

Imagine you're a bar owner who wants to make fancy cocktails, but you can't afford an expensive liquor license. You can do what many other bar owners in similar situations have done: liquor-less cocktails. Liquor licenses are expensive, but beer and wine licenses aren't.

Lenoir, a restaurant in Austin, does this. They have a non-liquor cocktail menu that instead features lower-strength ingredients like wine, vermouth, amaro, and sherry, which lets them avoid liquor license requirements. Premium Blend, an alcohol company in Florida, thrives in this loophole. They sell lower-alcohol imitation vodka, rum, whiskey, and tequila classified as fermented drinks rather than liquor. This puts them in the less-regulated wine category.

Different products = different rules, different risks, different opportunities.

TACO STREET AND POLITICAL RISK

People love regulating real estate. Zoning requirements, rent control, land use restrictions, tenancy laws, landlord laws, and construction requirements all impact how real estate is created, bought, rented, and sold. We have two sets of political risks: those that impact the real estate profession and those that impact the real estate market.

All real estate agents need real estate licenses. No license, no business. Anything that makes keeping a license harder is a problem. Given how long licensing rules have been around, I don't see them changing much.

When it comes to the market, I look out for rules that could reduce supply or demand. Observing the past decade, it's Texas's politics that make people come here in the first place. Low taxes and favorable laws create a vibrant and stable business environment where people can thrive. I could see a problem if Texas became more like California in its restrictions.

On the supply side, I look for zoning laws that restrict apartment construction. Restrictive zoning climates, like those in San Francisco, make building apartments nearly impossible. It's why we can't do business there. A few wealthy neighborhoods in Texas are like this, but I don't see this happening in every Texas neighborhood. I would instead bet that politics shift in favor of more, not less, housing.

Overall, I'm not too worried about our political risks. While we do exist in a highly regulated industry, the laws have been established for a long time. I don't see it changing much, nor do I see our markets becoming too restrictive on supply.

KEY TAKEAWAYS

· People use rules to manipulate your business environment. These rules can make doing business harder by making things more complicated, restrictive, or expensive. Know who these rule-makers are, the rules they're likely to change, and how you would be affected.

· Study similar businesses in other markets to see how rule-makers might tinker with your environment.

· You probably won't change the rules, but you can change which rules apply to you by changing how or where you do business.

EXTERNAL RISK CONCLUSION

You don't control your environment. You can't change your industry's risks, how markets shift, how the economy behaves, or the laws that govern you. Those things aren't your fault. But they are your problem. The world won't adapt to you. You must adapt to it.

You choose your industry and the industries you work with. You choose your markets by choosing what you buy and sell and who you sell to. These choices determine if and how you'll be impacted by economic shifts. You choose the rules that govern you by choosing where and how you do business.

Understanding what you control lets you choose and change your relationship to your business environment. This is how you will adapt to and thrive in environments you don't control.

However, even perfect environments don't guarantee survival. They only create the conditions where survival is possible. And if an environment is perfect for you, it's perfect for others like you.

PART 3: INTERNAL RISK

So far, we've looked at the world outside your business. Now it's time to look inside your business.

Think of your business as a machine. A machine is a network of parts and forces that converts inputs (energy) into outputs (more energy). A car is a network of parts (engine, tires, brakes, battery, transmission, etc.) and forces (gas, electricity, driver) that converts an input (gas) into an output (motion). Your business is the same: a network of people, parts, and forces that converts inputs (time, money, energy) into outputs (money).

As the business owner, you are its chief designer, engineer, and driver. You are responsible if it works or doesn't. The central risk in this section is that your business-machine breaks. So how might it break? And what can you do about it? The chapters in this section revolve around these two questions.

Building your business doesn't necessarily mean you understand how it works or why it would break. And just because you own your business doesn't mean you control it. The biggest risks involve ways you can lose control of your business without realizing it. Imagine Part 3: Internal Risk as taking your car to the shop to see what's broken and how to fix it so it doesn't break down in the middle of the road. Along the way, you'll find ways to build a better and more resilient business.

To do that we're going to look at your business from the following angles.

Business Model Risk will look at your business's blueprint.

Product-Market Fit Risk will take a unique look at how your personality influences the relationship between what you sell and who you sell it to.

Marketing Risk will look at where you market.

Competitive Risk will explain why competition isn't real and what to think about instead.

Operations is a four-chapter part-within-a-part that looks at how you solve problems **(Operations Risk)**, what you sell **(Product Risk)**, who you work with **(People Risk)**, and the tools you use **(Technology Risk)**.

Legal Risk will describe how the legal system can be used against you.

Cybersecurity Risk will look at ways you can defend against cyber-attacks.

Money Risk will look at how you make and spend money.

Along the way, we'll encounter a common trend. The default words and frames we use, such as "business model," "competition," and "marketing" are insufficient, misleading, or broken. Reexamining each concept will reveal better frames to help you make better decisions.

CHAPTER 10

BUSINESS MODEL RISK

Back in Chapter 6: Industry Risk, I mentioned working at a local apartment locating agency, Cool Apartment Agency. Here I'll tell their story and how it led me to going off on my own. Cool Apartment Agency was one of the best small-apartment locating agencies in town and a fun place to work. The agents were cool, and the culture was fun. After work we'd drink beer, play *Mario Kart* on the office Nintendo, and party together on the weekends.

It was a new agency, but they were doing great. Shortly after I arrived, they celebrated their best year ever: over $1.5 million in revenue, plus hundreds of five-star Google reviews. We were all proud. The owner, Andy, was ecstatic. However, when each of us agents put our monthly sales totals on a board, it became clear most agents were barely getting by, while a few (me included) were making the lion's share of the agency's income.

The model was simple. Cool Apartment Agency sent us leads. We closed those leads and split the commission once the deals closed. We got 60 percent, and the agency got 40 percent. Early on this was fine. I started off broke and made enough money to become not broke. But soon I got better at getting my own leads and closing my own deals. Eventually most of my money came from my own marketing. Despite this, Cool Apartment Agency kept taking their 40 percent split. This meant the more money I made on my own, the more money Cool Apartment Agency took—without adding any value.

This was a problem. Andy's incentive was to hire more agents to make him more money. The more agents he hired, the fewer leads each agent got. Our incentive as agents was to get our own leads and close our own deals.

I ran some numbers. I made around $10,000 from leads the agency sent me but paid Cool Apartment Agency around $30,000 from deals I closed through sourcing my own leads. *Fuck no,* I thought. I realized the better I got as an agent, the greater my incentive was to leave. That was what I did. I left to start Taco Street. The other top agents eventually figured out what I'd figured out: that they were better off leaving. The other agents couldn't make enough money off the insufficient leads they were getting.

Andy's Cool Apartment Agency had everything going for it. It was profitable, fun, had a strong brand, great people, hundreds of five-star reviews, and the perfect market. What it didn't have was a working business model. Unable to keep the people who made him his money, Andy shut down Cool Apartment Agency.

This next story is about another entrepreneur whose business model broke down, but for different reasons.

Malcolm Bradford is an alchemist. His superpower is magnetizing creative people and crafting unique experiences. Some examples include drum circles, ecstatic dances, pop-up art shows, and live music jam sessions. He even once built a disco tree house.

Malcolm decided it was time to alchemize his superpowers into a business. He found a perfectly drab warehouse and summoned the highest creative energy he could muster from himself and the people around him. After a monthslong sprint, his greatest creation, Flowmagin, was born. Flowmagin is hard to categorize. It was closer to a Burning Man camp than a gym or yoga studio. More than anything else, Flowmagin was a playground—the kind Malcolm always dreamed of.

It didn't take long to realize Flowmagin was a special place. The moment you walked in, you were bathing in a calm, serene energy. The walls were gradients of deep purple, pink, blue, and red hues, tastefully accented by warm lighting. There were flowing neon lights, fluffy chairs, cushioned columns, walls draped by silky curtains, and puffy cloud ceilings. Most impressive were the floors, which took three months to design. They were sturdy yet soft and bouncy—perfect for Malcolm's basketball-worn knees.

Flowmagin's event menu was a highlight reel of Malcolm's favorite activities. A typical week might have included ecstatic dances, open mics, drum circles, tea tastings, live music jams, pajama parties, breath-work ceremonies, sound baths, poetry slams, and Animal Flow yoga.

Everyone loved Flowmagin. Clients had a great time and formed a vibrant community. Instructors loved it. Flowmagin was the perfect canvas for them to bring their own creative callings to an excited audience. Everyone loved Flowmagin...except Malcolm.

From the moment Flowmagin was conceived in his mind, Malcolm never stopped. It took a firestorm of energy just to get it open. Once open, Flowmagin the playground became Flowmagin the business. Malcolm handled administration, hiring, training, cleaning, and coordinating events, all while struggling to make enough money.

Malcolm never took breaks. He had trouble letting go. "It was my baby. I felt like nobody would take better care of it than I would." Malcolm was plugged in and couldn't unplug. "I thought I could recharge by participating in Flowmagin's events, but I couldn't ever detach."

Eventually Malcolm realized the irony of what he created: a playground he couldn't play in. "I loved Flowmagin. But a small part of me also just wanted to step away and let it burn to the fucking ground."

He didn't do that. Instead, a few months after opening, Malcolm did what he needed to do to save himself and sold Flowmagin.

Risk = Damage x Existence x Exposure

DAMAGE: WHAT'S AT STAKE?

A business model is a network of incentives between you, whoever works with you, and whoever pays you. You (and any other owners) need incentives to keep the business alive. People who work with you—employees, freelancers, contractors, landlords, vendors, sponsors, suppliers, etc.—need incentives to work with you. People who give you money—customers, clients, investors, lenders, sponsors, affiliates—need incentives to give you money.

In our business-as-a-machine metaphor, your business model is your blueprint. Nothing is more foundational than your business model. Broken models become broken businesses.

Incentives glue your model together. Incentives are whatever makes people want to participate. Money is the obvious incentive. People do things because they get paid to. Less obvious incentives include passion, enjoyment, freedom, mission, purpose, or any non-money motive. Different people have different incentives. Some want more money. Some want more freedom. Some want passion projects. So on and so forth.

The key to any model is that it must work for everyone involved. If it breaks for one, it breaks for all.

There's a caveat. Some people are essential for your model, while some aren't. For example, say your business has a podcast. The company that sponsors your podcast is helpful, but your business won't fall apart if they leave. You are essential, but the sponsor isn't.

EXISTENCE: WHAT RISKS EXIST?

For anybody your model must work for, there exists a chance it stops working for them. This is the heart of **business model risk**.

List the people your model must work for. Include owners (yourself and partners), whoever works with you (employees, freelancers, vendors, suppliers, etc.), and whoever gives you money (customers, clients, sponsors, etc.).

Next, describe everyone's incentives and why your model would break for them. Note when you draw a blank. You have dangerous blind spots if you don't know why your model would or wouldn't work for somebody. Find out if you don't know.

Beware: *Should* work and *does* work are different things. Don't assume what should work will work. Andy at Cool Apartment Agency thought loyalty and friendship would be enough to keep the team together. It wasn't.

EXPOSURE: HOW LIKELY WILL YOUR MODEL BREAK?

Let's consider three angles: incentives, complexity, and personality.

Conflicting Incentives

You have incentives. Your essentials have incentives. Incentives conflict when you and your essentials want different outcomes. Say you have a legal problem you want solved immediately. You hire a lawyer and pay them by the hour to solve it. Their incentive isn't to solve the problem immediately but to work more hours so they can charge more money. You may want to grow as fast as possible, while your business partner wants a stable salary. The partnership will break because the incentives conflict.

At Cool Apartment Agency, it didn't matter that the model worked well for Andy, the agency's clients, and the apartment buildings that paid them. Andy's incentives conflicted with his agents' incentives. His agents were essentials for Cool Apartment Agency's model. Andy needed more agents to make more money. Agents needed more leads to make more money. When Andy recruited more agents, each got fewer leads, so agents survived by getting their own leads. Agents that got good at generating their own business didn't need the agency anymore and left.

Complexity

Imagine a road trip with friends. The more people in the car, the harder it is to find music everyone likes. Instead, you're more likely to play music nobody likes and everyone barely tolerates. Same goes for business models. The more people your model has to work for, the harder it is to please everyone, and the more likely it will break.

A simple model may need to work for just two people: you (the owner) and your customers. A complex model needs to work for more people, such as partners, customers, sponsors, investors, banks, employees, and landlords.

How do you know how complex your model is? Here's a trick. Explain your model to a friend. The longer it takes to explain, the more complicated the model.

Personality: Schemers and Martyrs

Your personal tendencies are the most interesting way to predict how your model will break. People skew toward one of two extremes. We'll call them **schemers** and **martyrs**.

Schemers focus on making their model work for themselves but not others. They focus on the money they can make, while other people's concerns are secondary.

Here are some signs you might be a schemer:
• Your team members keep leaving because you don't pay or treat them well enough.
• You lose customers and clients because they're not happy with you.
• Investors, sponsors, and vendors won't work with you because they're not getting the returns they need.

At the extreme, schemers become scammers, multilevel marketers, and pyramid schemers whose businesses better resemble clever theft.

Schemers aren't necessarily bad people. Andy was a good guy, but he behaved like a schemer. He focused on making his model work for himself more than his agents. That's why his agency fell apart.

Schemers survive until the scheme gets uncovered and people realize they're getting a bad deal. Professional schemers will close down, make a new scheme, and repeat the cycle.

Martyrs are the inverse of schemers. They make their business work for others but not themselves.

Here are some signs you might be a martyr:
• You work more than everyone around you.
• You're the first in, last out, leaders-eat-last type.
• You'll cut your salary and even run at a loss to help the business survive.
• You make customers happy, do great work for your clients, and treat your team well no matter what.

Eventually *you* won't survive. You'll have nothing left to sacrifice. You'll run out of money, burn out, and lose the will to go on. You'll die a hero's death, and nobody will be better off. Malcolm from Flowmagin was a martyr. His business worked for everyone but him, which was why he had to get out. Schemers and martyrs die for inverse reasons. Safety is in the middle. Your model must work for you and those around you, or it won't work at all.

Beware Middle Risk: It's tempting to think your model works when things seem fine. But what works today may not work tomorrow. Incentives change as people and their circumstances change. Given his success, Andy didn't see anything wrong with his model until it was too late. Time turned the cracks in his model into business-breaking fissures.

BUSINESS MODEL OPPORTUNITY

Any business model can work so long as it fulfills a few basic rules. Technology has been unlocking models that couldn't exist before. Most contemporary tech giants are successful because of business model innovations that created new ways to exchange value.

Airbnb turns ordinary people into amateur hoteliers. Uber lets anybody become a freelance taxi driver. Amazon, Shopify, and Etsy let people become online shopkeepers. Zoom lets yoga teachers run remote yoga studios. Substack turns people into independent news outlets. Podcasts let individuals become independent media companies.

You get the idea. You don't have to be a mega-sized tech company to create new models. All you need is some imagination to find new ways to create value for yourself and those around you. I'm currently enrolled in an online cooking school run by somebody who does marketing on Twitter, records videos on Zoom, and coordinates a community on a platform called Circle.

Complex models aren't necessarily a bad thing. Complexity lets you do things others can't. However, as a small business, you can't afford complexity the same way a big business can.

CHOOSING BUSINESS MODEL RISK

Never, ever think about something else when you should be thinking about the power of incentives.
—Charlie Munger (Warren Buffett's best friend and business partner)

Here are some ways you can approach creating a working business model.

Simplify the Model

As mentioned earlier, it's a lot easier to find road-trip music everyone likes when there are fewer people in the car. This is why few things are a more elegant and effective risk design protocol than choosing a simple business model. Simple models break less than complex models.

Simplifying means reducing the number of essentials your model needs to work for. For example, your model doesn't need to work for a landlord if you don't have a landlord. Your model doesn't have to work for investors if you don't have investors. Same goes with business partners, sponsors, employees, etc. Find the smallest number of people your model needs to work for, and go from there.

Change the Model

Change a model by changing incentives. That could be as simple as changing how people get paid. Andy from Cool Apartment Agency could have changed the agency's commission structure in a way that incentivized his best agents to stay.

Change the People

Instead of changing the model, work with people whose incentives match your existing model. Different people have different incentives. What works for one person may not work for another. Somebody who wants stable income will have different incentives from somebody looking for explosive growth. Bankers have different incentives from investors. Freelancers have different incentives from employees. Younger single people have different incentives from older people with families. Pick the right people for your model.

TACO STREET AND BUSINESS MODEL RISK

I didn't have to invent a new model for Taco Street. The apartment locating business model existed before me. All I did was tinker with it to fit my needs.

Here's how it works.

Me

I have to *want* to run Taco Street. That means making enough money to make it worth my time and having freedom so I can keep doing stuff I like. Otherwise I'll shut it down and do something else. So far so good.

The Apartment Buildings

Apartment buildings pay us commissions. They pay us because they need tenants. If they didn't need tenants, they'd stop paying, and we wouldn't survive. This is why market risk is so important. They're the weak link in the model.

Clients: People Looking for Apartments

Clients need to want to work with us. No clients, no money. This is easy. Our clients don't pay us anything. They get a free, helpful service. Our 140-plus five-star Google reviews are proof it works for them. Why clients work with us versus others is a story for a later chapter.

Freelancers

If it doesn't work for my freelancers, they won't work for me. I'll get stuck doing work I hate, burn out, and shut the business down. I've had the same freelancers for years because the work is consistent and pays well enough for them to stay.

Agents

I've hired and lost many agents because the model didn't work for them. Some couldn't handle the cash flow. Some didn't like the work (I'll get more into them later).

Unlike Cool Apartment Agency, I don't need other agents for Taco Street. I can make it work without them. In my experience, my model works best for people who can handle unstable cash flow and want freedom and flexible part-time income.

I'm not worried about our business model. I've found a good balance between making the model work for myself and making it work for others. It's simple. The incentives align, and everyone is happy with it.

KEY TAKEAWAYS

· Your business model is your blueprint. It is the network of incentives that aligns your motives with the people you do business with and the people who pay you.

· Win-win-win or die. Broken business models—those that don't work for the essential participants—become broken businesses.

· Know who is essential for your business to work and what their motives are.

· Use incentives to align motives so your essentials want to participate in your business.

· Don't be a schemer whose model works for you but not others.

· Don't be a martyr whose model works for everyone but you.

· Beware of complications. The more people your model has to work for, the more fragile it becomes.

· Know how you can change your model, simplify it, or change who it has to work for.

CHAPTER 11

PRODUCT-MARKET FIT RISK

Zach Horvath was surrounded by thirty of his closest friends and family. Together they were celebrating the latest product launch for his company, Live a Great Story. For months, Zach and his team designed, tinkered with, and workshopped subscription accountability journals. The idea was simple: help people disconnect from technology and write down their goals.

Zach hoped the journals would propel Live a Great Story from a local lifestyle brand into a multimillion-dollar lifestyle juggernaut. People loved the idea. Feedback was overwhelmingly positive. Zach went all out on marketing. His team emulated famous Kickstarter campaigns; grew a big, engaged email list; shot compelling videos; and built intricate online sales funnels. Zach poured tens of thousands of his own dollars into online ads. They had a product people loved, a marketing machine ready to fire, and an engaged audience waiting to buy. This launch party was to celebrate a *fait accompli*.

Zach clicked launch and waited for his bet to pay off. He waited...and waited.

"Within five minutes I knew it was a failure," Zach later said. The swelling support he sensed never materialized. Sales were terrible. "We had thirty people there surrounding and congratulating me for launching a new product, and inside I'm devastated."

Zach's project had everything except product-market fit. Instead of celebrating with his friends and family, he was wondering how he would save his company from total collapse.

Consider another story. Michael Kane is a quintessential Dungeons and Dragons dungeon master. His arms are art galleries covered with fantasy figures crafted over the two decades he's guided people through epic quests and mystical fantasies that go on for years.

Being a dungeon master requires a lot of manual craftwork to visualize scenes and characters. Michael wanted something he could use to make campaigns easier to run and more visually satisfying for his players. So he tinkered. He drew up some prototypes, partnered with some artists, and created tabletop tokens for heroes, monsters, landscapes, and other things one might encounter on a DnD campaign. Such was the beginning of his new company, Geek Tank Games.

Michael put a few hundred dollars into a Kickstarter campaign to sell his new tabletop tokens to see if anybody was interested. It turns out a lot of people were. Geek Tank Games' first campaign spread like wildfire and raised over $60,000.

Michael was ecstatic. He had a product-market fit bull's-eye. His second launch sold out too. Michael knew he was on to something but knew he had to find outside help when it came to marketing. So he partnered with professional marketers and tripled down for a third campaign. Together they shot professional videos, crafted social media ad campaigns, and found influential partners. This third launch raised over $300,000 in pre-sales. Between pre- and post-launch sales, Michael's Geek Tank Games had made over a million dollars.

This was the peak before the fall for Michael's Geek Tank Games. I'll tell the rest of his story later in the book.

Risk = Damage x Existence x Exposure

DAMAGE: WHAT'S AT STAKE?

You already know what product-market fit (PMF) is. Either people buy your shit or they don't. If they do, great. If they don't, you're screwed, and it's game over. This is **product-market fit risk**.

It's obvious when you don't have it. You're not selling enough. What isn't obvious is *why*. Even if you do have PMF, it's worth understanding how and why you wouldn't have it in the future.

PMF is tricky because it's a two-sided problem: is it the market or the product? Are you selling the right product to the wrong people? Are you selling the wrong product for the right people? Or are you just screwed, selling the wrong thing to the wrong people?

How would you even know?

EXISTENCE: WHAT RISKS EXIST?

PMF applies to everything you sell. Zero PMF is obvious. Nobody is buying. It's like selling drugs at a convent. You wouldn't even try. Total PMF—like selling drugs at a techno rave—is also obvious. No worries there.

Beware Middle Risk: Middle Risk is the most dangerous PMF risk. It's when you think you have it, but you don't. Positive signs will seduce you. You'll get great feedback. People will book sales calls. Enthusiasm will be strong. People will say they'll buy when it's launched. Media coverage will be exciting. So you'll invest more and more, thinking you're on the right track.

And then when it comes to launch...crickets. Your so-called enthusiasm won't manifest. Sales calls won't close. Reviews will be tepid. Subscribers will cancel. Customers and clients won't return. The project will flop. And the worst part is you won't know why. This was Zach's problem. He had fans and supporters but not buyers. But this still doesn't answer the question. How do you know if it's the product or the market?

EXPOSURE: HOW LIKELY WILL YOU NOT HAVE PMF?

Let's look at two angles: verification and tendencies.

Verification

PMF is either verified or not: you either know you have it or you don't. How do you know? Money! People pay instead of saying they'll pay. Customers return. Sales calls close easily. Subscribers stay subscribed. Clients book more sessions. Word-of-mouth referrals grow with time. Michael *knew* he had PMF because people were actually buying his products.

More signs, less risky. Fewer signs, more risky.

How do you figure out if you have a market or product problem? There's no exact science, but knowing your tendencies is a good place to start.

Tendencies: Product People versus Market People

You fall on a spectrum. You skew toward being either a **product person** or a **market person.**

Product People: Superpowers

You love making *the thing.* You pour your heart and soul into making the best shit possible. Think of masterful storytellers, painters, artists, chefs, product designers, programmers, inventors, and engineers. You tinker, tinker, and tinker some more until *the thing* is perfect.

Michael from Geek Tank Games is a classic product person. Before starting the company, he had been a Dungeons and Dragons dungeon master for more than two decades. "With Geek Tank, I just wanted to make something that I would buy," Michael explained.

Product People: Super Problems

You like making but not selling. Sales feels icky. It pairs with words like *manipulative, bothersome,* and *harassing.* Self-promotion feels more like attention-whoring. This was Michael's problem. He loves making things but hates marketing. "I didn't want to be another person spamming people asking for money," he explained.

As a product person, you secretly have *Field of Dreams* fantasies. *Build it and they will come! Word will spread and you'll be rich!* Maybe they will. Maybe you'll make something so good it can't be ignored. Maybe you're like the podcaster Dan Carlin from *Hardcore History* who can get millions of listeners despite no self-promotion and a shitty website. If not, the fantasies won't manifest. You'll build, but nobody will come, and you'll give up. You'll be some hidden-gem artist nobody will discover until long after you're dead.

Market People: Superpowers

Market people are the inverse. They like to sell *the thing.* They focus on how much money they can make. They're return-on-investment-calculating spreadsheet wizards, A/B testing advertising alchemists who master turning clicks into dollars, persuasive copywriters who know which words convert sales, super-connected socialites plugged into the best networks, channel specialists who know where their audience is and how to engage them, email list builders who sustain audiences for years, engaging videographers who make compelling bite-sized Instagram stories, branding strategists who design their way into people's minds, and fast-food juggernauts who know which store locations will drive the highest revenue.

Market People: Super Problems

Market people can't tell and may not even care if their product sucks. They're slumlords renting out rat-den apartments, fake-smiling real estate agents on bus stop benches, and personal injury attorneys on highway billboards. They're the clown-faced get-rich-quick YouTube schemers and the people stuffing your email's spam inbox. They're click-bait news websites, manipulative sales agents, Instagram influencers shilling scammy cryptocurrencies, and Hollywood executives mutilating old classics.

Zach from Live a Great Story is a market person. He's great at building sales funnels, picking market channels, connecting to his audience, and creating awesome videos. In the case of his failed launch, product was his problem. He created something his audience didn't want.

What about you? Are you more of a product or a market person? If it isn't obvious by now, think about what you spend the most time on and what gets you the most excited.

PRODUCT-MARKET FIT OPPORTUNITY

If I had asked people what they wanted, they would have said faster horses.
—Henry Ford.

Product-market fit is the entrepreneurial holy grail. When you have it, money finds you rather than the other way around. Because he had PMF, Michael was able to quickly turn a few thousand dollars into a million-dollar business.

Great innovators don't wait for PMF. Nobody asked for the Ford Model T, the internet, or the iPhone. Innovators create, and other people catch up. Finding PMF before others do is like being the first one to find a goldmine.

There's no ceiling for something with the right product and market. It's the nuclear fusion of the business world. *Game of Thrones, Harry Potter,* and *The Lord of the Rings* were all great enough to sell well as books. When brought to screens by studios and paired with marketing juggernauts, they became permanent parts of the world's culture. Apple became one of the world's most valuable companies by pairing great products with the greatest marketing any technology company ever accomplished.

Knowing your tendencies—if you skew more toward product or market—means you're that much closer to learning how to find PMF.

CHOOSING PRODUCT-MARKET FIT RISK

If you don't have or are worried you don't have PMF, here are some steps you can take.

Verify: Don't mistake enthusiasm for PMF. Money is truth. Find out if people will pay you or not.

Pivot: If you don't have PMF, get it! You can do it the cheap way with some slight tinkering or the expensive way with a total overhaul.

Change the Product: Sell different products. Zach's business could have collapsed after his failed launch, but it didn't. Soon after the launch, he leveraged the marketing assets he'd built and pivoted back to selling his original products, all of which had proven PMF. The next months would see him break old revenue records and save his business from disaster.

Tinker the Product: Can you make slight adjustments to your existing product? Can you make cheaper or more expensive versions? Can you afford to change the price?

Change Markets: Can you sell the same thing to different people?

Change Both: Can you change the product and market? This is what Scribe Media did. They made a cheaper version of their flagship service for a different market.

Cover Your Blind Spots

If you're a market person, learn how to make better products. If you're a product person, learn marketing. Of course, that's easier said than done. If this isn't realistic, partner with somebody who has the traits you don't have. Your combined powers will be greater than the sum of each.

Michael knew marketing was his blind spot, so he partnered with marketers who were good at what he wasn't. It's why he was able to jump from a $60,000 Kickstarter campaign to a $300,000 campaign.

TACO STREET AND PRODUCT-MARKET FIT RISK

It's obvious we have PMF. Client calls are easy. I can turn total strangers into excited clients in minutes. We have a ton of great reviews, repeat clients, and plenty of referrals. Nothing to see here...right? Not exactly. Writing this chapter made me look at myself.

I'm a product person. I like making stuff way more than selling stuff. For better and worse, I've been the kind of person who spends months or years working on a project but shies away from marketing. In retrospect this is why many of my past projects didn't work. I made but didn't sell.

For reasons I'm exploring with my therapist, I hated the idea of sales and avoided it for as long as I could. Only desperation led me to ironically build what is effectively a sales and marketing business.

In retrospect, being a product person was an advantage. Almost all real estate people are market people who focus entirely on sales and self-promotion while sucking at their job. I came at the business from the opposite angle. I didn't want to sell people into working with me.

I wanted people to *want* to work with me. That's why I designed Taco Street to feel like a unique experience rather than a transactional service.

KEY TAKEAWAYS

· Product-market fit or die. You cannot build a business unless you sell something people pay for.

· Beware false PMF. Just because you think you have PMF doesn't mean you do.

· The only way to verify you have PMF is by getting people to pay you.

· Even if you have PMF, understand why you may not in the future.

· Observe your behavior. If you focus on product, you may have a market problem. If you focus on the market, you may have a product problem.

· Cover your blind spots. Lean into what you don't normally do, or partner with somebody who does what you don't.

· Determine a few ways you could change your product, market, or both to get PMF.

· PMF doesn't guarantee survival. It only exposes you to the next problem.

CHAPTER 12

"COMPETITIVE" RISK

"Jesse, I don't know how you guys did it, but you were profitable this year."

This could have been an ordinary meeting between a business owner and his accountant. But this wasn't an ordinary owner, business, or time. The owner was Jesse Cole. He owned a baseball team. The year was 2020.

Social-distancing protocols shrunk their stadium capacity by two-thirds and choked off their main revenue source. Jesse couldn't make money throwing concerts either. Making things harder, Jesse had slashed their sponsorship revenue. Despite all that, they—a sports team in a pandemic—were profitable.

How?

Jesse doesn't own a major- or even minor-league baseball team. He owns a collegiate-level team in a league you've probably never heard of. But his team isn't any ordinary team. Jesse Cole is the owner of the Savannah, Georgia-based Savannah Bananas. If you haven't heard of them, you're in for a treat.

On the surface, the Bananas are an ordinary baseball team. Zoom out and you'll see a normal baseball game: pitchers, batters, fielders, etc. Zoom in and you'll see anything but ordinary. On any given day, you may see batters walking out to music pro-wrestler style, a five-minute wedding ceremony, infielders singing karaoke while fielding ground balls, senior citizen cheerleaders, a breakdancing first-base coach, players wearing kilts, batters with flaming bats, or a pitcher on stilts.

Then there's Jesse. He isn't off in some distant skybox like a Roman Emperor during a gladiator match. Jesse is more circus ringmaster than sports team owner. He's running around the stadium in his quintessential banana-yellow tuxedo, cheerleading, screaming, and getting the crowd fired up.

Then there are the fans. They aren't there to network with clients or watch until boredom sets in. You'll see dads, moms, seniors, kids, and teenagers all having a blast. The games are so popular they've been completely sold out for years. When the pandemic brought the Bananas to the brink of disaster, it was their rabid merchandise-buying subscription-service-ordering fans who flooded the Bananas with money to keep them alive.

Risk = Damage x Existence x Exposure

DAMAGE: WHAT'S AT STAKE?

Since we're on the topic of baseball, let's talk about it. Baseball is a competition. One team plays against another according to a predetermined set of rules. Whoever fulfills those rules better (scores more runs, in this case) wins. The winner gets the trophy. Hooray. All competitions have this dynamic: fixed rules, fixed number of participants, clear winners and losers.

Now think about competition in business. When do you play a game with a fixed set of rules directly against another business? When are you awarded a prize after winning a game?

Go ahead. I'll give you time.

Having trouble? Have you ever rock-paper-scissored another business for a customer? Have you ever seen cotton-candy-haired coffee baristas maul each other for the pleasure of serving you your morning latte? Have you ever presented your sales pitch to another company to see who gets the client? Have you shopped your product to rivals to see who wins a customer?

No. No, you haven't. Nor will you ever. In business "the trophy" is a human. Humans have agency. *People choose the "winner."* Imagine a World Series where one team wins more games, but the fans give the trophy to the other team because they're more fun to watch. Of course that would be absurd, but so is using the word "competition" in a business context.

That's because in business, **competition isn't real.**

Let me say it again for dramatic effect.

Competition isn't real.

In a competition, you play the same game directly against someone else. In business, we're all playing *different* games *next* to each other.

Imagine two bars next to each other. One serves fancy cocktails to worldly and sophisticated gentlefolk (like this author), and the other serves cheap beer to those deprived of class, taste, and budget. Even though they're neighbors, they aren't competitors. One is playing the fancy cocktail game, and the other is playing the cheap beer game. People who want fancy cocktails won't choose the beer bar and vice versa. The risk isn't being "beaten" by a "competitor." The risk is *not being chosen.* In other words, the risk is being *replaced.*

That's why competitive risk is actually **replacement risk**. Not only is competition not real, but even thinking about it is hurting you. Trying to fit in and do what everyone else does may be safe socially, but it's a terrible business risk. Worrying about competition focuses your attention on what other businesses are doing instead of what your customers and clients want. This leads to copycatting. It's why almost all businesses and people in all industries look and act exactly like each other. It's why nail salons, law firms, real estate agencies, corporate consultants, minor-league baseball teams, Instagram life coaches, health food brands, yoga studios, coffee shops, and sports bars all look and act exactly alike.

Once you notice it, you'll see it everywhere. This is insane when you think about it. Why would anyone choose you if you're just like everyone else? Without a good answer you'll default to the worst option: price.

Enter the Commodity Problem

You sell lovely bunches of coconuts for a dollar. Your neighbor sells lovely bunches of coconuts for a dollar. Each of you gets half the customers.

You drop to 99 cents, and you get all the customers. They drop to 98 cents, and they get all the customers. You drop. They drop. The cycle continues. You're locked in a price war. Unless one of you murders the other, both of you will price-reduce your profits away. This is a strange death.

Technically, you can stay "in business" and continue selling coconuts. But you don't control coconut prices. The market does. When you don't control pricing, you don't control your business. In effect, when you commoditize, you're not even a business anymore but a *profitless employee to a market you don't control.*

Price is a commodity's only distinguishing factor. Big Walmart-type businesses can play that game. They have the size to buy and sell at cheaper prices than you can. This is why small mom-and-pop shops that tried to play the commodity game with Walmart all went out of business.

EXISTENCE: WHAT RISKS EXIST?

You can be replaced directly or indirectly. **Direct replacement** is when you're replaced by similar businesses. Take Netflix. You can replace it with other streaming services like Hulu, Amazon Video, and YouTube. The Savannah Bananas can be beaten in a baseball game but can't be replaced because there is no other experience like them in town.

Indirect replacement is replacement by anything else. You can replace Netflix directly with other video streaming services or indirectly by going to the bars, walking your dog, plotting the perfect murder, yoga, or anything else you can occupy time with. This is another reason competition is a broken frame. "Competition" focuses your attention on direct replacements. In reality, there are more indirect replacements than direct ones.

Fans can indirectly replace the Bananas by watching sports at home, playing video games, and going to the gym, but because the games are so fun, they don't.

What about you? Describe ways you can be replaced directly and indirectly.

EXPOSURE: HOW REPLACEABLE ARE YOU?

The more you can be replaced, the more you will be replaced. You're on a spectrum between totally replaceable (commodity) and irreplaceable (monopoly).

Signs You're a Commodity

When you're a **commodity**, you have to find money. You resemble similar businesses. People price shop you with similar options. Potential customers and clients keep choosing similar alternatives. Deep down, you kinda know. Even you don't buy the bullshit story about why you're different. The harder you try to convince people you're different, the more likely you're not.

Signs You're a Monopoly

When you're a **monopoly**, money finds you. You are the only option. Sales calls are easy. You don't have to fight hard for customers. People pay your prices without question. Word of mouth spreads. People go out of their way to work with you.

REPLACEMENT OPPORTUNITY

The less you can be replaced, the less you will be replaced. Monopolizing is a survival strategy as much as it is an opportunity to not have to struggle to differentiate yourself. It's a chance to keep more clients, build a loyal customer base, and get free marketing through word-of-mouth referrals.

Changing the frame from competition to replacement is also optimistic. You can't do what Amazon does, but Amazon can't do what you do either. You can create human experiences that big businesses can't. The Cheesecake Factory can't make a Michelin-starred restaurant. Small entrepreneurs can. Major League Baseball can't have a ridiculous banana-themed baseball team. Jesse Cole can.

CHOOSING REPLACEMENT RISK

You don't control other businesses, customers, clients, or alternative options. You can control how you can be replaced.

Jesse knew his team couldn't just be another generic Wildcats or Bulldogs sports team. They had to be unique. The name was a good start, but people still needed a reason to come out and watch baseball—a notoriously slow and boring game. Why do that when they could sit home and watch professionals play from a comfy couch in an air-conditioned room?

Jesse couldn't just recreate the same old baseball experience. Instead *he looked outside the baseball industry.* His inspiration came from people like Walt Disney and P.T. Barnum—entertainers. What resulted was the world's first and only baseball circus. And people loved it. It's why the Bananas don't have fans but fanatics who bought merchandise and subscriptions to the Bananas' new streaming service that helped keep them profitable during the pandemic.

So what about you?

You're not big enough to "campaign finance" yourself an artificial monopoly (i.e., cable companies, utilities, the NFL, etc.), nor are you a murderous mafioso gunning down rivals. Monopolizing naturally is your only option.

Can't/Won't

Monopolize by doing things others can't or won't do in ways your clients care about. Nobody had the capacity, imagination, and audacity to pull off what Jesse did with the Bananas. Nobody could have brought the same blend of baseball expertise and manic circus energy to baseball like he could.

Take a few minutes to write down a few things you can/will do that others in your industry can't/won't.

"A" and "The"

A means being one of many. *A* barbecue joint. *A* sports bar. *A* nail salon. *A* law firm. *A*'s are commodities.

The means owning or topping a category. *The* is a monopoly. *The* only

Egyptian barbecue joint in Texas. *The* only supplement company featured on that famous podcast. *The* best cocktail bar. *The* swankiest nail salon. *The* most exciting, beautiful, coolest, fun, etc.

Write down ways you already are or can become *the* in categories your customers would care about.

The Ultimate Monopoly

Everyone gets one freebie monopoly: reputation. Your reputation is the relationship you have with the people you do business with. It can't be replaced, replicated, or taken away. Reputation is why word of mouth spreads, how you get referrals, and why people don't question your prices. It's why people go out of their way to work with you and buy your stuff. Jesse and his Bananas have a strong reputation within their community, which is why their fans wanted them to survive.

How would your best customers and clients describe your reputation?

Stacking Monopolies

One monopoly is nice. More is better. The more monopolies you stack, the less replaceable you'll be. For example, *the* best barbecue joint with *the* best beer selection with *the* prettiest views of the countryside.

For *the* Savannah Bananas, they are *the* most fun event in town. *The* only banana-themed baseball team. *The* only baseball circus. *The* only team with a crazy yellow-tuxedo-wearing owner. *The* only small team with hundreds of thousands of fanatical social media followers. You get the idea. If you're struggling for ideas, do as Jesse did, and look outside your industry for inspiration.

Describe the stack of monopolies you have. What is one way you can grow it?

TACO STREET AND REPLACEMENT RISK

When I got into the apartment locating business, there were lots of people and established businesses in the market. How could I survive?

It didn't take long for me to realize a few things. Most locators either suck at what they do or work as faceless representatives behind generic company brands. Most don't know the market well and focus entirely on closing deals rather than adding value. It's why so many people have had terrible experiences with locators.

When I left my old agency and went off on my own, I knew I had to stand out to survive. Why would anyone work with me if I was just like everyone else? My stroke of genius came when I was eating at one of Austin's best taco trucks. My mind quieted as the fatty, juicy, spicy *al pastor* danced around my taste buds. "What a wonderful town this is!" I mused. "Tacos everywhere! Food trucks! Restaurants! Bars! Breweries!"

It seemed every street had tacos.

Street tacos...

Taco Street.

My eyes bulged. The world slowed. It was so obvious. Was I really going to have a taco-themed real estate company? Fuck yeah, I was.

That's how Taco Street Locating—*the* only taco-themed real estate company in the world—was born. I wasn't just another body behind some soulless real estate brand. I was the face of my own ridiculous taco-themed business. With my own business, website, and silly brand, I could tell my story and turn what typically felt like a human-to-business experience into a human-to-human experience.

That wasn't enough, of course. My service needed to stand out. Otherwise clients wouldn't stay loyal. Most locators (and most service professionals in general) are trained to sell first, and help later. The logic is simple: *If I help you, you won't need me, and you won't hire me. Hire me, and then I'll help you!*

I did the exact opposite. I was going to help first, and sell later. I wrote detailed blog posts and recorded YouTube videos so people could learn what I knew. Then I designed a research process unlike anything else. Each of my clients gets comprehensive and personalized spreadsheet reports. Clients love them because they save lots of time. Nobody else does this because it's a huge pain in the ass (how I do this at scale is a topic for a later chapter).

This might seem counterintuitive. Why would anyone hire me when they could get all this research for free? Simple. People hire me because they trust me. They trust me because I help them more and faster than anyone else does. I hear it from clients all the time.

Your guides were so useful!

I watched your videos!

This spreadsheet is amazing!

You helped my friend find an apartment!

I love this whole Taco Street thing you have going on!

It shows in my Google reviews. I have *the* most for any independent locating business in town. Speaking of Google, why would someone hire us instead of just using Google? I can't do what Google does, but Google can't do what I do. Google won't make you super detailed spreadsheets, drive you around town, or buy you tacos. I will.

In sum, I have *the* only taco-themed apartment locating company. For hundreds of clients, I am *the* only apartment locator they trust and refer their friends to. I have *the* most comprehensive apartment research process and *the* most useful guides. Most importantly, I'm *the* only me. People want to work with me because they like me as a person.

All this has helped make Taco Street less replaceable, but not irreplaceable. There are still many competent locators, big companies with more resources than I have, and other ways of finding apartments.

KEY TAKEAWAYS

· You have no competition—only replacements.

· To survive, monopolize in ways your clients care about so you become less replaceable—and ideally, irreplaceable.

· Monopolize by owning or dominating as many categories as possible.

· Don't copy similar businesses. Find inspiration outside your industry. Do things others can't or won't do.

· Invest in and protect your most valuable monopoly: your reputation.

CHAPTER 13

MARKETING RISK

Joe Speiser raised a bunch of money to start an online pet food company called PetFlow. The strategy was simple: build a big audience and sell them pet food. PetFlow did that by making and sharing cute animal content on Facebook. The strategy worked...better than Joe could have ever imagined. Their videos were going viral, and their audience was growing exponentially.

Soon Joe realized he was on to something much bigger. Selling pet food online was nice, but it didn't scale like media did. Nor was it as fun. Joe saw an opportunity and pounced. He doubled down by creating a new media company called LittleThings that focused on viral feel-good stories. It didn't take long for them to find a winning formula.

"We became masters at harnessing Facebook's news feed with feel-good articles, videos, and stories," Joe said in a series of tweets.[2] LittleThings grew fast. In a few years, one employee became a hundred, with a New York City office and a live video studio. Everything was amazing. They were growing like crazy and making millions each month. Their viral Facebook videos were key.

"We built the business on the backs of Facebook, drinking from their firehose of eyeballs," Joe said.

Facebook even invited LittleThings to their corporate headquarters to feature them as a star media company.

---

2 Joe's Tweet Storm: https://twitter.com/jspeiser/status/1641073771120414722.

And then things changed. Perhaps preferring rage and chaos, Mark Zuckerberg, Facebook's CEO, overdosed on LittleThings' mushy, feel-good content.

So Facebook changed the algorithm. It wasn't the first change Joe saw, but it was the most dramatic. "I watched helplessly as 90 percent of our organic traffic from Facebook dried up. If we wanted more traffic, we would have to pay for it through sponsored ads." LittleThings had a BigProblem: almost all of their traffic—and therefore, money—came from Facebook. Without that traffic, LittleThings couldn't afford payroll, their office, or their live studio anymore. "It was a death sentence," Joe said.

Timing couldn't have been worse. Joe was weeks away from selling LittleThings for a hundred million dollars. Instead, Joe had to let go of the team and wound up selling his company for a fraction of what he would have gotten otherwise. All because of an algorithm change.

Risk = Damage x Existence x Exposure

DAMAGE: WHAT'S AT STAKE?

Marketing is how you connect to people who pay you—whether it's your audience, customers, affiliates, clients, or sponsors. In this chapter I'll assume you have product-market fit, so we won't look at what or how you market but *where* you market.

Where you market is where you reach your customers. We'll call these **marketing channels**. You can't survive if you can't reach the people who pay you. It's like losing your connection to your oxygen tank when you're scuba diving underwater.

Marketing risk is when you get cut off from your market. There are all sorts of channels. There are old-school low-tech channels like door-to-door sales, flyers, billboards, direct mail, networking events, retail storefronts, and word of mouth. Then there are modern high-tech channels like Facebook, TikTok, Google, Airbnb, Amazon, YouTube, and Instagram.

Enter Crackhead Marketing

Crack dealers have a simple business. They lure people in with free samples. Customers try the crack, love it, and come back for more. They get hooked and ruin their lives by spending all their money on crack. *Cha-ching!* It's a splendid recurring revenue model.

Modern marketing channels are the same. Their "free samples" are easy setups, instant market reach, and quick-easy money. "You get the benefit of instant access to millions, and fast growth," Joe said, explaining his experience with viral content. It seems too good to be true. Your complex digital alchemy turns money into more money. Just do more, and you'll be rich...right?

"We were addicted to the Facebook volume of traffic, and no other source could move the needle," Joe said. You spend more and more money getting high off amazing returns. The more you use, the more money you make, and the more dependent you become.

Like LittleThings, you are now a full-blown **crackhead marketer**. Maybe you're lucky and this strategy works forever. More likely something goes wrong, such as an algorithm change, which is what happened with LittleThings and Facebook. That's only the beginning.

Other crackhead marketers flood the market while the platform's artificial-intelligence-optimized bidding-war algorithms raise prices and bleed everyone's profits dry. Maybe your campaigns simply lose effectiveness. Platforms can introduce new rules and restrictions that force your business to fit their mold—a common problem with Airbnb hosts. Maybe you used a naughty word, broke some rule, or were the victim of an ordinary glitch. Platforms can suspend your accounts without cause or recourse.

When it happens, you'll desperately bang on the door of apathetic customer service agents representing apathetic digital drug-dealing employers. If you're lucky, it won't be a big deal. If not, as it was for Joe and LittleThings, you'll watch helplessly as your business withers away.

The worst part is these digital crack dealers have the perfect negotiating position. They know you need them more than they need you. They know how much traffic they send you, the money you spend, the returns on your investment, and what others are willing to pay. In effect, you're playing poker against somebody with infinite money who can see everyone's hand. Maybe losing the channel won't be a big deal because you have other ways to reach your market. But if you're like many modern businesses, the platform is your only channel.

You hop from platform to platform, launching, tinkering, and optimizing campaigns, chasing the quick high of fast money, only for the cycle to repeat. Or you'll wind up like LittleThings: fucked. Sure, maybe this works in the short term. But in the long term it's like trying to build a village on land that has earthquakes every month.

"Can you ever truly sleep well at night knowing at any time [your business] can all be taken away with just a simple algorithm change?" Joe warned.

EXISTENCE: WHAT RISKS EXIST?

Channels that work can break. Foot traffic can drop. Social media platforms can ban or suspend you. Campaigns can lose effectiveness. Flyers can be torn down. Platforms can raise prices beyond what you can handle. Word of mouth can dry up. Google can cut traffic to your website. A stupid pandemic can ruin your in-person marketing events.

EXPOSURE: HOW FRAGILE IS YOUR MARKETING?

Your connection to your market is foundational. The more that foundation shifts, the bigger your problem. Let's look at it in three ways: concentration, the channel's age, and whether you own the channel or not.

Beware Concentration Risk: Your marketing is either concentrated in a single source or spread across multiple channels. A less-concentrated business might have five marketing channels where no channel takes up more than 40 percent. LittleThings was hyperconcentrated. Over 80 percent of their traffic came from Facebook. The more concentrated you are, the more dependent you are on that channel—and the more fragile your business is.

List your major marketing channels and what percent of your business comes from each. If you don't know, find out.

Old versus New Channels

How much do your marketing channels change? Old low-tech marketing channels like paper mail, billboard advertising, door-to-door sales, and in-person networking rarely change. New high-tech marketing channels change all the time. Prices change dynamically, and rules change. The more you rely on older channels, the fewer changes you'll likely see, while the more you rely on modern channels, the more changes you'll likely see.

Owned versus Rented Channels

All channels are different in terms of how they work and how much you control them, but they are all either owned or rented. **Rented channels** are pay-to-play or follow-the-rules-to-play. This is all social media and tech platforms. Typically they're owned by big corporations.

Their risks become your risks. They have their own incentives and motives. They care more about themselves than they care about you.

If screwing you over helps them survive, they will do it. They are the drug dealers who can cut you off from your market at any time for any reason.

If you're a single-rented-channel business, like an Airbnb host who only uses Airbnb or an e-commerce store that only uses Amazon, you're not a business. You're a freelancer to a marketing channel you don't own or control.

Owned channels are the opposite. You own and control access to your market. You can't be blocked, suspended, or price gouged out of them. Your website, email newsletter, and podcast are a few examples. Reputation is the ultimate owned channel. It's yours. It's free. It generates word-of-mouth business. It can't be canceled or copied.

The problem is that owned channels are hard to grow. It takes a while to get website traffic, a big email list, an audience, and a strong reputation. It's a lot easier to get seduced by the instant numbers from major platforms. But the more business that comes from owned channels, the safer you are.

What about you? Do you rely on older or modern marketing channels? How much of your business comes from channels you rent versus those you own?

MARKETING OPPORTUNITY

Every channel you aren't using but could be is an opportunity. New channels expose you to more people and increase the odds you find new markets. Modern marketing channels, as much as I've shit on them, have made it easier than ever before. Using modern marketing channels is like having an army of algorithm-powered super-soldiers working nonstop to connect you to the people who want to find you. They can help you grow in ways nothing else can.

If nothing else, opening new channels buys you relief from the anxiety that comes with relying on a single channel. But most importantly, owning your marketing channels means creating a stable and secure way of reaching your customers that can't be taken away. Owning your channels is an opportunity to own your business.

CHOOSING MARKETING RISKS

If you don't control your marketing channels, you don't control your business. Don't abandon modern marketing channels, but don't let them decide your fate. Don't rely on a single channel. Instead, spread risk across multiple channels. That could be a new Instagram page, YouTube channel, or more industry-niche channel.

New channels could mean older marketing strategies like direct mail, flyers, and in-person networking. Even if you don't control it, older channels are less cancelable than modern channels are. In the long term, survival means having channels that can't be taken away. This includes your email list, your website, and, most importantly, your reputation. These take a while to grow.

Joe knew LittleThings was in a fragile position but never managed to decouple from Facebook. "We tried for years to diversify by pushing hard into [other marketing channels]. We were never able to grow the alternative channels big enough to balance out the insanely large amount of views Facebook was sending," Joe said.

Take a few minutes to describe ways you can reduce your reliance on any single channel. List a channel you can open and how you can increase ownership of your marketing in the long term.

TACO STREET AND MARKETING RISK

Early on, I got most of my business from a single channel. It worked great. Leads were cheap, and deals closed fast. I made a ton of money.

It felt like cheating. It worked so well I stopped using all other channels. Apparently, the platform felt it was cheating and banned my account. It felt like getting caught with my pants down.

Leads dried up, and I freaked out. No leads would eventually mean no business. It was obvious I couldn't put myself in that position. I spent the next few weeks opening new channels. This helped, and I was able to turn the lead faucet back on. But I still had work to do. These new channels could break just as easily as the old one.

After that, I got more aggressive. I focused on channels I either owned or had more control over. I got a Google business page, a YouTube channel, and, most importantly, my own professionally designed website where I could create blog posts. Early on, they didn't do much, but over time, more and more of my leads started to come from those channels.

With a client-based business like mine, I benefit from a survivor's bias. The more clients I work with, the more repeat and referral clients I get in the future. These days, most of my business comes from my website, referrals, and repeat clients.

Overall, I still have a lot of marketing-channel risk. I still depend on a lot of channels I don't control. But with time my website will continue to be a bigger lead source, and more of my business will come from referrals and repeat clients.

KEY TAKEAWAYS

· **Live by the channel; die by the channel.**

· **Don't worship fickle gods. Don't put your fate in the hands of modern marketing channels. Realize the same channel that gives you life can take it away at any time.**

· Diversify across multiple channels. Don't overlook older channels. In the long run, create your own.

· Own your marketing, own your business.

CHAPTER 14

OPERATIONS RISK

"This is your last chance!" the boss threatened. "If *one* piece of candy enters that room unwrapped, you're *fired!*"

Thus began one of the most famous scenes in the classic sitcom *I Love Lucy.*

Lucy and her friend Ethel were working at a candy factory. Their job was wrapping candy as it came along a conveyor belt. "Let her roll!" the boss commanded as candy started coming in. It started off nice and slow. Their confidence was high.

"This is easy!" Lucy said as candy trickled in.

"Yeah! We can handle it!" Ethel responded.

They wrapped and wrapped some more. All was well. Slowly, the conveyor belt sped up, bringing more candy. Lucy wrapped faster and faster, but they couldn't wrap fast enough. Confidence turned to panic.

"Ethel, I think we're fighting a losing game!" Lucy yelled.

Chaos ensued. Unable to keep up, Lucy and Ethel resorted to eating and stuffing whatever they couldn't wrap down their shirts and into their hats in a desperate attempt to keep their jobs.

Poor Lucy!

Risk = Damage x Existence x Exposure

DAMAGE: WHAT'S AT STAKE?

Operations are the network of people and technology that solve the problems your business is designed to solve. It doesn't matter how amazing your product is, how much clients love it, or how great the market is if you can't execute on operations.

In a nutshell (or candy wrapper), this scene in *I Love Lucy* describes all operations ever. Operations have two sides: first there are incoming problems (here it's candy that needs wrapping). Then there's problem-solving (candy-wrapping) capacity. Problem-solving involves people and technology—in this case, Lucy and Ethel who wrap candy, and the conveyor belt that brings the candy to be wrapped.

If incoming candy is at or below Lucy's candy-wrapping capacity, she'll be fine. If the conveyor belt breaks, Lucy won't have incoming candy to wrap. If incoming candy speeds up beyond what Lucy can wrap, as it does in the scene, Lucy will be overwhelmed, and chaos will ensue. **Operations risk** is when you can't solve enough incoming problems.

EXISTENCE: WHAT RISKS EXIST?

Your business is just like Lucy's candy factory. Selling stuff (products or services) creates incoming problems. You have products to make and deliver, services to fulfill, expenses to track, taxes to pay, and marketing campaigns to support. Then you have to solve those problems with people and/or technology. For every incoming problem, there exists a chance that it won't get solved.

EXPOSURE: HOW FRAGILE ARE YOUR OPERATIONS?

Here's a new concept: the Lucy Ratio. The Lucy Ratio describes the relationship between incoming problems and problem-solving capacity. The top of the Lucy Ratio represents incoming problems. The bottom represents problem-solving capacity.

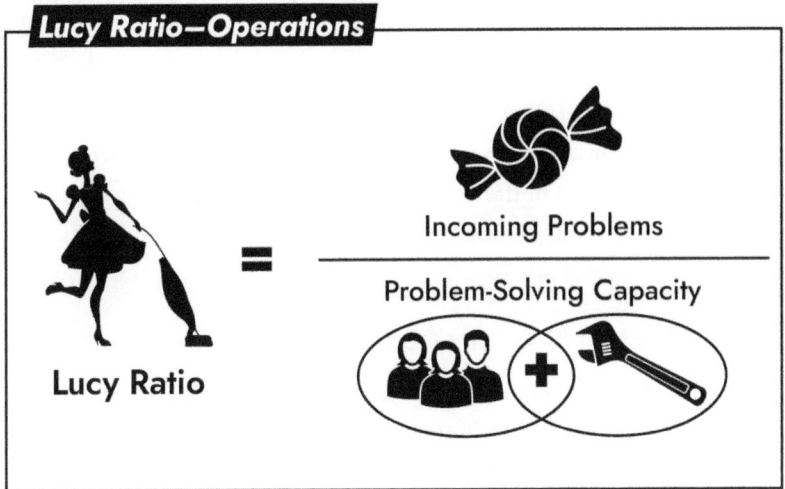

A Lucy Ratio below 1 means your business can solve the problems coming in. The lower the ratio, the safer your operations are. A ratio above 1 means you're giving your business more problems than it can solve. The higher the ratio, the more fragile your operations are.

Beware Compound Risk: It usually isn't one problem that will hurt but the accumulation of many.

If you've ever waited way too long for food at a restaurant, you know what operational meltdowns look like. It's rarely one big problem but a bunch of small things breaking down at once. The oven breaks. Food spills. A cook calls in sick. Servers don't come to your table. The kitchen can't put out food fast enough. Food comes out late, cold, or undercooked. Servers take forever to bring checks. You sit there waiting, wondering what the fuck is going on.

Everyone is miserable. Employees get overwhelmed. Customers get pissed and leave shitty reviews. If this goes on long enough, employees will quit, and people will stop eating there. Eventually they'll shut down. Good operations function more like Amazon Prime: simple, quick, and seamless. Everyone is happy.

The next three chapters explore why operations break down. On the top of the Lucy Ratio, you overload your business with too many problems (**product risk**). On the bottom of the ratio, the people who solve problems stop solving problems (**people risk**) and/or the tools you use break (**technology risk**).

TACO STREET AND OPERATIONS RISK

Early on, I saw a common trap with other apartment locators. They could juggle ten to twenty clients without much fuss. Beyond that the wheels would fall off. They'd get overwhelmed. There were too many clients, details to remember, communications to juggle, research to do, and invoices to manage. Inevitably they would burn out and quit.

To survive, I needed to figure out how to handle more clients, offer better service, and stay sane. If I didn't, I would end up like them.

KEY TAKEAWAYS

- Operations are how your business solves problems and makes money.

- Operations break down if your business can't handle incoming problems.

CHAPTER 15

PRODUCT RISK

As a trade school graduate, Lukas Wells worked a few blue-collar jobs before starting a home services company, Good Property Services. Lukas was eager to start. He took on plumbing, electrical work, tree work, handyman work, landscaping, flooring, painting, drywalling, insulation, and anything else he could get his hands on. He couldn't stand the idea of saying no.

He got off the ground and made money fast. But it didn't take long for things to go south. Every job needed different tools, people, and skill sets. Schedules were hard to manage. Projects kept getting delayed. New tools were becoming more expensive than the jobs they were worth. Invoicing became too complicated. His messy spreadsheets couldn't handle the complexity. Worse, he ran most of the business through his phone.

His operations couldn't keep up. "It was like getting kicked in the mouth," Lukas said. "We flooded a client's kitchen twice and could have burned another's house down with bad electrical work." The house didn't burn down—but Lukas did. Months of watching projects go wrong and the stress of flirting with financial disaster was too much. Lukas burned out. Rather than close down, Lukas found a full-time job and went part time with Good Property Services.

Risk = Damage x Existence x Exposure

DAMAGE: WHAT'S AT STAKE?

Your business makes money because it sells products and/or services. Everything you sell creates a downstream set of problems to solve. Products have to be made, shipped, and accounted for. Services require working with clients. If you can't solve those incoming problems, your operations will break down, and you won't make money. This is **product risk**. Like Lukas, you'll burn yourself out trying to juggle everything.

EXISTENCE: WHAT RISKS EXIST?

Everything you sell triggers a set of tasks. Think about it as a recipe. Somebody orders a lemonade. You mix sugar, lemons, water, and ice. Pour it into a cup. Serve.

Every step in every recipe can fail. The lemons can get moldy. The juice squeezer can break. The girl working the squeezer can quit. Sugar can spill. Water can get contaminated. Cups can get lost. The same goes for anything you sell. Every step creates a failure point.

Write up a process recipe for one of your routine tasks as if you were handing it off to an assistant. Note how long the recipe is and how each step along the way may go wrong.

EXPOSURE: HOW LIKELY WILL STEPS FAIL?

Let's look at ways you can overload your operations from two angles: volume and variety.

Volume: The more you sell, the more problems you have to solve. Fewer sales, fewer problems.

Variety: The wider the variety of products you sell, the wider the variety of problems you have to solve. A lemonade stand selling lemonade and orange juice is simple. Both are basically the same process. A lemonade stand selling lemonade and pizza is much different. Both products have wildly different ingredients and steps. More variety, more problems.

Combined, you have the volume variety matrix.

High-Volume – Low-Variety: *Taco truck, lemonade stand.*

Low-Volume – Low-Variety: *Fine art sales, luxury real estate sales.*

Low-Volume – High-Variety: *Consulting agency.*

High-Volume – High-Variety: *The Cheesecake Factory.*

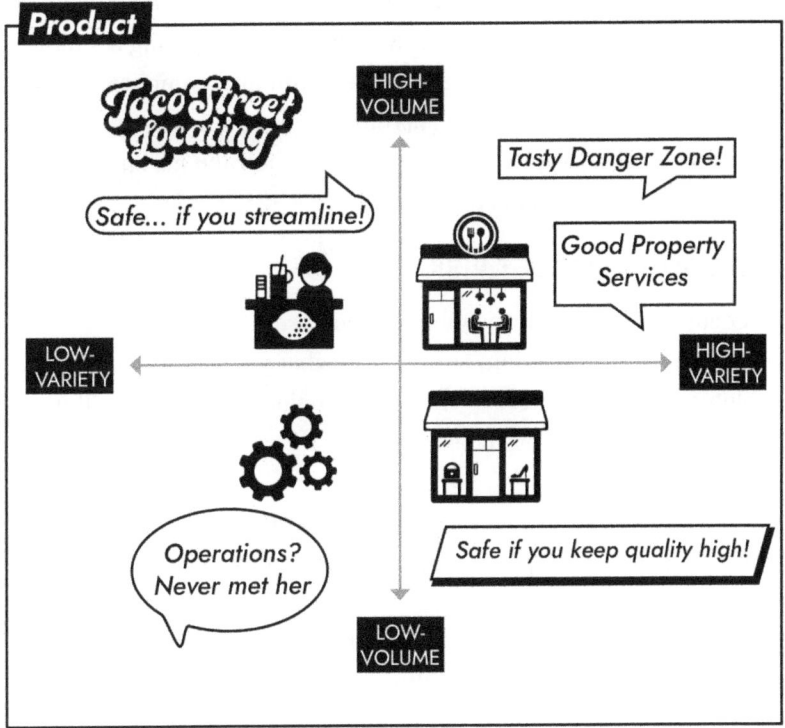

If you're not familiar with the Cheesecake Factory, the apex of luxury suburban megamall dining, all you need to know is that they have a twenty-one-page menu with 250 different items. It's glorious. **The Cheesecake Factory** is the pinnacle of operational complexity.

For a small business like yours, the first three quadrants are doable. The Cheesecake Factory quadrant is not. This was Lukas's problem. He Cheesecake Factoryed his operations to death with a high volume and variety of problems to solve.

Where are you on this volume-variety matrix?

PRODUCT OPPORTUNITY

Simple scales. It's way easier to grow a business when you're solving the same problems over and over. Simple is sane. Running a simpler business is easier and less stressful than running a complicated one. Slimming down and streamlining his offering saved Lukas's sanity along with his business. Despite working a full-time job and his business on the side, he's never been happier.

CHOOSING PRODUCT RISK

You choose what you sell and what you don't sell. Nothing will improve operational risk better than simplifying what you sell. Having fewer problems—or having more of the same problems—means you'll need fewer people and simpler tools.

"I dramatically cut our service offerings. These days, painting and remodeling take up 80 percent of our work," Lukas said.

Pick variety or volume—not both. The Cheesecake Factory you are not. If you're finding yourself overwhelmed, pick one product or service you could cut, and describe how that would ease your operations.

TACO STREET AND PRODUCT RISK

One of the most important decisions I made with Taco Street is deciding what we don't do. We don't buy, sell, fix, flip, wholesale, work with private landlords, or do commercial real estate deals. We *only* do apartment locating. Narrowing even further down, we primarily deal with higher-end luxury apartments to avoid getting bogged down by higher-work, lower-commission deals.

Apartment locating is a high-volume business. We close over a hundred deals a year. Offering other services on top of apartment locating would overwhelm my operations and risk burning me out. Being a high-volume, low-variety business means we're solving many problems, but the same problems over and over again. Designing operations around it was easy.

It's also why I could grow Taco Street into other cities. I didn't change anything. All I did was copy-paste our existing operations into new markets.

KEY TAKEAWAYS

· Nothing impacts your operations more than what you sell.

· What you don't sell is just as important as what you do sell.

· Don't overwhelm your operations by giving your business too many problems to solve. Cut products and services that create more problems than they're worth.

CHAPTER 16

PEOPLE RISK

Back to Cool Apartment Agency. Andy, the owner, had a talented assistant, Jordan. She did everything. She onboarded new agents, managed invoices, kept the office clean, ran errands, closed deals, and took care of whatever miscellaneous tasks people threw her way—all while going to programming school.

It was great...until it wasn't. Jordan did what many smart, competent people did: found better-paying work. Jordan's tasks reverted back to Andy. Now he had to onboard, manage invoices, keep things clean, do miscellaneous tasks, work with his own clients, and run the agency. On top of that, he had to find a replacement for Jordan.

Weeks went by as interviewees came by the office with no luck. Weeks became months. One day a new hire came in. The new assistant was smart, competent, and friendly. She was soon up and running and doing a great job...until she did what other smart, competent people did and found a better-paying job. Andy was back to square one.

Risk = Damage x Existence x Exposure

DAMAGE: WHAT'S AT STAKE?

People solve problems. Otherwise you wouldn't hire them.

I want to focus on what I'll call the **Swiss Army knife problem**. Swiss Army knives are great. They can cut, saw, poke, slice, screw, open cans, and even uncork wine bottles. People like Jordan are Swiss Army knives. They're reliable, trustworthy, and they can do lots of different stuff. You give them stuff to do, and they do it well. So you give them more stuff to do. They do that well too. They solve a bunch of different stuff. Everything is amazing.

However, unlike Swiss Army knives, people have agency and can leave. When they do, you're screwed. All of a sudden, the problems they were solving aren't getting solved. Their work becomes a game of tasky hot potato. Whose job is it now? Yours? Other people's? Anybody's? Then you have to find a replacement, which means interviewing, figuring out who's bullshitting you, hiring, training, and hoping that the new person works out. If they don't, you have to do it all over again.

This was Andy's problem. The problems his assistant solved weren't getting solved anymore. There wasn't anybody else in the agency who could take over, so the work kept reverting back to Andy. Eventually the added pressure (along with a broken business model) led to him closing the agency.

EXISTENCE: WHAT RISKS EXIST?

People who work with you can stop working with you. This goes for employees, business partners, freelancers, and contractors. Sometimes it's your fault. You picked the wrong person. Maybe you even picked the right person but failed to train, pay them enough, or set proper expectations. Or maybe you burned them out with too much work.

Sometimes it's not your fault. Shit happens. People can leave for any number of unexpected reasons: family emergencies, health complications, alien abductions, random life circumstances, or better job opportunities. Either way, even if it's not your fault, **people risk** is your problem.

EXPOSURE: HOW SENSITIVE ARE YOU TO PEOPLE LEAVING?

We'll look at this from three angles: happiness, difficulty, and where knowledge is stored.

Happiness

Unhappy people don't stay in jobs for long. How do you know how happy someone is? *They're fine! They're totally happy!* you may be feeling. You can guess or you can know how people feel. The less you know, the more likely you will be taken by surprise.

Difficulty

The harder someone's job is, the harder they will be to train, the more likely they will fail, and the harder they will be to replace. At risk of stating the obvious, fewer people can do harder work, while more people can do easy work. Difficulty depends on depth and breadth. Depth is anything that requires a deep knowledge, such as engineering or accounting. More depth, more complexity.

Breadth comes with variety. The more variety of tasks you give someone, the harder their job becomes. The harder somebody's work, the harder they will be to replace. This was Andy's problem with Jordan. None of her individual tasks were difficult, but the variety of them made her role harder to replicate.

Rented versus Owned Knowledge

Here's the big one. When you hire somebody, you rent their time, knowledge, and capabilities. When that person stops working, you lose their time *and* their knowledge.

When the knowledge required to run your business lives outside your business, your business is more fragile. When people leave, it is harder to replace their knowledge and capabilities.

On the other hand, when you document somebody's knowledge, you turn **rented knowledge** into **owned knowledge**. What this means is that the knowledge it takes to run your business now lives inside your business in the form of documentation. The more your business's knowledge lives inside your business, the safer your business is.

You're probably thinking about someone in your business you would hate to lose. Imagine them leaving. How much would it suck? What would you do after they left?

PEOPLE OPPORTUNITY

Let's take a look at some upsides to bringing new people into your business.

More Genius Resources

$1 + 1 > 2$

Other people can do things you can't. Hiring means renting someone's time but also their genius. See what magic unfolds when you mix new flavors of genius together. When Michael Kane, the product-oriented dungeon master from the Product-Market Fit Risk chapter, partnered with marketing-oriented professionals, he was able to multiply the success of his Kickstarter campaigns.

Access

In school, having other people do your work is cheating. In business, it's smart. These days the internet and remote work mean there are endless numbers of people all over the world who are ready, willing, and capable of doing your work for you.

Appreciation

People get smarter over time. The longer they do a job, the better they get at it. Their gains become your gains.

More Problem-Solving

The more problems your business solves, the more money it can make. Alone, your business is limited to how many problems you can solve. Adding other people means your business can solve more problems and make you more money. Hiring also lets you reduce your personal work input while increasing what your business can do overall.

More Time and Energy

Most importantly, hiring buys your time and energy back. That means more vacations, more time with friends and family, more time to relax, more hobbies, and less risk of burning out.

CHOOSING PEOPLE RISK

Choosing people risk is about who you hire, how you train people, how you assign work, and how you store knowledge. Here are a few ways to tackle your people problems.

Hire the Right People

Yeah, yeah. Easier said than done.

This isn't a "how to hire" book, so I'll keep it simple. The people you hire have survival criteria the same way you do. You need money, time, and energy to survive. So do they. Make sure what they need matches what you can offer.

Talk to Your Team

You can guess or you can know how somebody is doing. How do you find out? Ask! Have real human-to-human discussions with the people you work with. Try this simple and totally not awkward conversation starter:

Hello, fellow human. Are your needs being met? If not, what can we do about it?

Simplify Work

You don't control people, but you do control the work you give them. The harder you make someone's job, the more likely they will fail, and the harder they will be to replace. The easier you can make somebody's job, the more likely they will succeed, and the easier they'll be to replace.

Redundancy

Train multiple people to do the same work. The more people know how to do something, the better. That way, one can slot in for another when needed.

Build Your Business Cookbook

Rented knowledge comes and goes. Instead, own your knowledge by building a **Business Cookbook**.

Your Business Cookbook is the collection of recipes it takes to run your business. Document process recipes so new people will be easier to train. This can be as easy as writing stuff in Word documents or recording yourself explaining things. Start with stuff you know, and then move on to your team. The more you document, and the more you update it, the safer you'll be.

Give this a shot. Describe one way you can simplify somebody's job. Try documenting, in written or video form, one process it takes to run your business.

TACO STREET AND PEOPLE RISK

Taco Street wouldn't be possible without other people. My team takes on the boring, menial work that would otherwise burn me out. Taco Street the business works over a hundred hours a week, but I personally only work a small fraction of that.

I built a process I call the Big Fancy Spreadsheet that compiles my apartment research for each client into a single document. It takes hours to make, and it's a pain in the ass, but clients love it. It's a huge reason they work with us and give us great reviews. There's no way I could do it myself. I'd burn out in an afternoon. So I hired freelancers.

But I didn't just hire one freelancer. I hired four. That way, if one, two, or even three can't work, I'll still be fine. The added speed is nice too. I haven't made a spreadsheet in years. Same goes for invoicing. Hundreds of deals means hundreds of invoices to make, send, follow up on, and follow up on some more. Since spreadsheet making and invoice management are similar processes, I trained my phone team to manage invoices too. They swarm invoices like piranhas and speed up how quickly we get paid. It's amazing. Another freelancer only manages advertising campaigns. It's super monotonous, but it's critical for lead generation. My freelancers have been happy with the work. They get consistent work that pays well. I haven't had to replace any of them in years. One even invited me to his wedding.

I hire companies for specialist work like bookkeeping, accounting, and web design because companies have built-in redundancy. When my original accountant left his company, there were others there ready to take his place. It was like nothing ever changed.

On the other hand, my track record with hiring other apartment locating agents has been terrible. Here's how they've all panned out:
- Sasha couldn't make enough money fast enough and took a salaried job.
- Rebecca was a great agent but left the business to resolve mental health issues.
- Anna was smart but never followed up with clients and hated sales.
- Michelle's husband got a job in a new city, and they both relocated.
- Rob left for another agency weeks after joining.
- Sara worked with me for a year and then ghosted me.
- Harold was my best agent until he found out his wife was cheating

on him, filed for divorce, and left the state to rebuild his life.
• Katy left the business to become a schoolteacher.

As of this writing, I only have one part-time agent as backup.

Taco Street doesn't *need* other agents to work. However, this means I'm still the one making most of Taco Street's money. This is one of my biggest vulnerabilities.

The only thing everyone I hire has in common is specialization. Nobody has more than three different tasks. My phone team only does phone calls and data entry. My advertising guy only manages advertising. Agents only work with clients. My accountants only do accounting. This makes everyone's job easy, which makes hiring and training simple.

Early on, I got tired of training people. So I documented everything needed to run Taco Street in our Business Cookbook. I wrote documents and recorded videos explaining how to do everything. These days, all I have to do is send somebody a link to a specific process recipe in the Cookbook, and they're ready to go in no time. Overall, hiring has let me work with more clients and make more money, all while saving my time and energy.

KEY TAKEAWAYS

· **People are hard.** They have feelings, complex lives, mixed motives, and difficult-to-determine levels of competency.

· **People are amazing.** They can bring things to your table that you never imagined and unlock exciting new opportunities.

· **Whenever you work with people, their blessings and curses become your blessings and curses.**

· Pick well. Train well. Give people the right work. Talk to your team.

· People come and go. Turn rented knowledge that lives outside your business into owned knowledge that lives inside your business by building your Business Cookbook.

CHAPTER 17

TECHNOLOGY RISK

White Armor was a weapons and armor manufacturer out of Kharkiv, Ukraine. Well, sorta. They weren't making drones, rifles, missiles, or tanks to shoo off pesky neighbors. White Armor was closer to the twelfth century than the twenty-first. They made crossbows, helmets, breastplates, greaves, and other such goods one might encounter in a medieval-themed fantasy role-playing game. They were more renaissance festival than military industrial complex.

Making the armor were master Ukrainian blacksmiths with decades of experience. The blacksmiths wanted to enter the US market, where the real money was. Stas, a Ukrainian living in Texas, was helping them. He was the perfect partner. Stas was fluent in both Ukrainian and English, experienced in business, and more than comfortable with fancy technology. Stas would bring the blacksmiths from the twelfth century to the twenty-first.

Stas got the blacksmiths up and running in no time with an Etsy page and a Facebook account. Hardcore live-action role players and renaissance festival fanatics were salivating. Orders besieged White Armor's inbox. Lots of orders and master-level craftsmanship meant lots of complexity. This wasn't some one-size-fits-all party-store garbage. White Armor's blacksmiths were masters. They had a craft they loved and a reputation to protect. Everything had to be perfect. That meant satisfying everyone's unique specifications and measurements.

"Everything is tailor-made to fit your size, eye position, body type, and fighting manner," their Etsy page boasted. They made things like German sixteenth-century crossbows, fluted and articulated Gothic combat steel elbow cops, evil *Lord of the Rings*–style gauntlets, English plate arms, full-body Italian-Gothic cuirasses, and Corinthian helmets.

Running White Armor's digital armory meant tons of materials to order, timelines to meet, measurements to take, customers to communicate with, shipping labels to print, and expectations to manage. It was a complex logistical dance. To organize everything, Stas implemented a CRM (customer relationship management) software to run it all. The CRM became White Armor's central nervous system. Everyone relied on it. White Armor's store became popular, and reviews started piling in.

"Simple isn't the word I would use to describe White Armor. Well-made and fit to order, good communication from the seller keeping me within the loop. Great value for the money I spent, and I don't regret it. They fit well on my arms/shoulders. 10/10. Would buy again," one reviewer said.

Everything was going well...until one day, Stas woke up and couldn't get into the CRM account. Something was wrong, but he didn't know what. Everyone was effectively locked out of the business. Stas couldn't get a straight answer from the CRM's customer service agents. Making things worse, the blacksmiths in Ukraine lost their internet connection at the same time. It was an operational one-two punch.

Orders kept coming in, but nobody could see them or communicate with customers. Details were lost. Customers were left in the dark. Timelines were thrown in the air. The blacksmiths freaked out. They were more comfortable with thousand-degree forges than business software.

Given Stas's background in business technology, he wasn't a stranger to technological meltdowns.

"You always know something is going to break. You just don't know what, when, and for how long," Stas reflected. Still, it was a pain in the ass. He had dozens of people to keep in the loop. "I figured the CRM would come back soon. I just didn't know when. Days? Weeks?"

If that wasn't bad enough, all this was happening at the same time Stas was going through the messy part of a divorce. All Stas remembers feeling was a long, drawn-out *fuuuuuuuuuuuck*.

The outages didn't last long. The internet came back soon, and they were able to get back into their system a few days later. It turned out they were on the wrong side of some technical glitch. "It could have been much worse," Stas said. "We didn't lose a lot of money, but this tiny glitch took us weeks to recover from."

Risk = Damage x Existence x Exposure

DAMAGE: WHAT'S AT STAKE?

Technology solves problems. Otherwise, we wouldn't use it. These days we use more of it than ever. Even simple businesses are becoming cyborg-like networks of superpowered technology. Which is great. We can solve more problems, hire fewer people, and run more efficient businesses. Most of us wouldn't be the entrepreneurs we are without it.

But our operations can become a technological house of cards, one break from collapse. It's easy to forget how much we rely on it. There's the obvious stuff we use every day, like our phones, laptops, and sales software. Then there's the stuff we forget about, like electricity, internet, our laptop's operating system, mobile apps, laptop chargers, the email system powering our marketing campaigns, our payment processors, and the fancy tools connecting different software together that we take for granted. Only when it breaks do we remember it even exists.

It's old technology too. An old colleague organized his entire business on a paper notebook. This notebook contained tens of thousands of dollars' worth of relevant client details. He never worried about it, assuming he'd never lose it. Whether he understood it or not, he was choosing to risk his entire business database on something that could get lost at a coffee shop.

It's not just the number of tools but each tool's complexity. Software is built on mountains of code crafted by fancy-pants programmers. Machines are complex networks of parts and forces. Anything can break for any number of reasons that escape our understanding.

Fixing stuff may not be easy. You know where to fix a car. But software? You may have no idea where to begin. And that's if you can even tell it's broken. It's easy enough to spot a flat tire, burst pipe, or clogged toilet. But software problems might be invisible. It's hard to spot something that goes wrong inside of lines of code. Things can break without us even realizing it. By the time we notice, the damage may already be done.

Sometimes we get cute. We're seduced by fancy Bluetooth-enabled smart-home lightbulbs, fingerprint-scanning door locks, machine-learning soap dispensers, rocket-scientist-engineered air fryers, voice-command vacuum cleaners, artificially intelligent robot copywriters, and bells-and-whistles-loaded sales software. In reality, all we're doing is buying ourselves more problems. What seems fancy is actually fragile. When things break, we spend more time fixing problems than running our businesses.

Then there's the reality that we don't own many of the tools we use to store critical files, organize customers, handle payments, manage projects, launch marketing campaigns, send invoices, and track cash flow. This is often in the hands of companies we don't own or control. Their risks become our risks.

The wrong tools may even put you in a hostage situation. Companies can leverage the roles their software plays in your business to extract more money. What this means is that our businesses are run on top of a large, complex, and potentially fragile house of technological cards that we don't own or understand.

So what do we do about it?

EXISTENCE: WHAT RISKS EXIST?

Tools that work can stop working. This is **technology risk**. We'll refer to all the tools you use as your **technology stack**. Imagine each tool as a card in your metaphorical house of cards. Let's split your stack between software and hardware.

Physical tools can break or get lost or stolen. This includes stuff like your laptop, phone, chargers, headphones, microphones, car, internet connection, machinery, toilets, air conditioning, notebooks, door locks, and water heaters.

Software can get buggy or become too complex or too expensive to maintain. This includes the code behind your computer's operating system, your phone's apps, your website and its plugins, as well as the software you use for accounting, invoicing, marketing, payment processing, email, and project management.

Every physical piece of hardware and line of code in software is a break-point. Supposedly beneficial "updates" can become Windows Vista–style dumpster fires that make things worse. The company powering the software can go out of business. Like a messy spreadsheet, tools can become too complex to handle.

Tools don't even have to break. They can become more expensive. Your "I can't believe it's this cheap" $25-per-month sales software is now a

$200-per-month subscription you can't get rid of. Software can even turn against you. Payment processors are notorious for withholding money. In 2022, a leaked memo revealed PayPal's plans to grant themselves the right to take up to $2,500 from people's accounts for "spreading misinformation."

Let's look at how complex your tools are and who owns them.

Complexity

Total complexity depends on the total number and complexity of each individual tool. The more complex something is, the more fragile it is.

Compare a lemonade stand to a brewery. The lemonade stand uses simple technology: lemon squeezer, mixing bucket, ice machine, water fountain, wood plank retail stand, chalkboard, milk crate chair, and glass jar to collect money. Easy stuff. Easy to fix. Easy to replace.

A brewery uses grain mills, measuring tools, mash turnerizers, fermentating contrapulators, gizmo beer-a-trons, alcohol containment chambers, hydro boilerators, and mass bottling whatchamacallits. In the taproom they use beer taps, payment processors, a TV for sports watching, and Wi-Fi for remote-working laptop warriors. In its entirety, a brewery is technologically complex. Hard to understand. Expensive to fix. Expensive to replace.

Tool Complexity

Complicated tools break more than simple tools. A Bluetooth air fryer is more likely to break than a cast-iron pan. A car engine is more likely to break than a hammer. Simple small business software is less likely to break than complex big-business enterprise software. Complex tools tend to be more expensive to fix than simple tools. Complex tools require complex parts and complex people. From a technology standpoint, the brewery is more fragile than the lemonade stand.

Rented versus Owned

Some tools you own, like your laptop. Most tools you rent. You're probably not building your own sales and invoicing software. Luckily, software tools aren't as monopolistic as social media platforms. You have more choices. The more your operations rely on rented software, the more your operations are in the hands of companies you don't own or control.

TECHNOLOGY OPPORTUNITY

The more problems you can solve, the more money you make. Building the right technology stack is like having an army of cheap algorithm-powered problem-solving soldiers at your disposal. What used to take employee-filled departments now just requires a few people with the right tools.

These days there have never been more, cheaper, and more powerful tools to choose from. It's like walking into Home Depot where every tool can make you richer. The options get better every year as companies pour trillions of dollars into research and development. Learning new tools is like discovering new superpowers. What used to take years of software training now only takes imagination, a few YouTube tutorials, and the will to experiment. Keep an eye out for tools you could be using, and discover new superpowers you never imagined. Who knows what opportunities will be out there as we enter the age of artificial intelligence.

CHOOSING TECHNOLOGY RISK

Choosing Technology Risk is about choosing the right technology. This is easier than you may think. The same way you can read restaurant reviews on Google and Yelp, you can read software reviews on websites like Capterra. Same goes for hardware.

Here are a few things to look for when picking tools.

Avoid Bad Tools

The best way to avoid technology risk is to avoid shitty tools. It's a lot easier to pick the right tool from the beginning than remove a shitty tool once your operations are up and running.

Do your research before implementing business tools. Avoid technology with a bad reputation. Otherwise you'll buy yourself problems you never wanted. For example, don't use payment processors that have a reputation for holding money hostage.

Beware Complexity

Complex technology requires complex people to figure out, work with, and fix. The simpler the tools you use, the easier it is for you and anybody you work with to use them.

Check if They Allow Data Export

Don't let companies hold your data hostage. Choose tools that let you export your data. Tools that don't can effectively hold you hostage to extract more money.

Check for Good Customer Service

Customer service is the most common software complaint. Software is complicated. Odds are you're not going to fix it yourself. This is a nonobvious reason renting software can actually be a great thing. When you rent software, you also rent the company's customer service team. In effect, their staff becomes your staff. When those tools break, you want quick, friendly, and competent support staff to fix your problems. This is the difference between solving a problem in hours versus days.

Change Tools

Different tools, different risks. Replace bad tools with good tools.

Simplify

Do you really need that nuclear-powered artificial-intelligence-optimized soap dispenser? Or will the manual pump do just fine? Sometimes less is more. Cut out tools that create more problems than they solve. Know when simpler is better.

Go through your technology stack and single out any weak points. These are the "it would suck ass if that broke" tools. What would you do if that tool broke? Do you have somebody on call to fix it? Can you buy a backup option? What tool can you switch to in case it breaks?

TACO STREET AND TECHNOLOGY RISK

I'm obsessed with technology. There's no way in hell I could run Taco Street without my tools. Early on, using sales software was my biggest advantage over other locators. I could handle more clients and make more money while preserving my energy.

It's my most important tool. I've stuck with the same sales software for years, but if worse came to worse, I could export my data from my current sales software into another in a few hours. I almost had to do that when the text messaging system inside the software broke, and another time when the software company accidentally changed my monthly plan from $25 a month to $500 a month. Fortunately, their support staff helped me resolve those problems without much fuss.

When I left my old agency, I used simple website and design tools to launch the first version of Taco Street without hiring professionals. Each tool's customer support staff was super helpful in resolving problems along the way.

Virtual phone software let me build my own remote call center and invoicing department. Pairing that with affordable freelancers let me operationalize our service in ways nobody else could. Tools like Zapier let me glue together different software. Combined, everything has let me create interconnected and streamlined operations. None of this needed any coding. All I had was my imagination and the will to tinker. This is why I can run Taco Street from a laptop on my kitchen counter while only working a few hours a week.

This is all well and good. But one time, fancy turned against me. I once lost around fifteen thousand dollars' worth of leads because of a spam filter. The software I used to send leads from my marketing funnel to my sales software stopped working. Normally I would have gotten an email notification for each lead, but the spam filter intercepted them. Instead, leads piled up in the background for weeks without me realizing it.

My car that I use to meet clients costs thousands each year in maintenance. Other than that, everything else is straightforward. Keeping Taco Street simple means I don't need a lot of technology. Almost everything else has simple backups or alternative options to use.

KEY TAKEAWAYS

- You are a technology company whether you realize it or not. Use it, but don't take it for granted. What works today may not work tomorrow.

- Pay attention to the most important tools that run your business. Look out for any weak points.

- Get excited about tinkering with technology, but don't overcomplicate things with tools you don't need.

- Choose the right tools by doing your research. Don't let anyone hold your data hostage.

CHAPTER 18

CYBERSECURITY RISK

Drew Binsky has been everywhere. He's been to every country in the world and every US state. He's no stranger to scary situations. Drew's been arrested, harassed, chased by police, interrogated by Russian police on North Korea's border, involved in a deadly bus accident, nearly kidnapped, and trapped in riots.

But one of his most terrifying experiences began in the unlikeliest of places: on the back nine of a pristine Wisconsin golf course. Drew was with his dad when he received one of the scariest messages of his life. *Your YouTube channel has been hacked,* the text message read.

YouTube was everything for Drew. He's amassed one of the most impressive video travel libraries ever compiled. His channel has hundreds of videos and millions of subscribers. What began as a hobby morphed into a business with seventeen team members that he supports through YouTube revenue.

"Aside from a family death or health scare from a loved one, this was the worst thing that could happen. Seven years of pouring blood, sweat, and tears into making content and building a community was everything to me. To see it go in the blink of an eye...it still makes me anxious," Drew said.[3]

Googling made the anxiety worse. He read countless horror stories of people waiting weeks or months to get their channels back—if they ever

3   https://www.youtube.com/watch?v=QNBQkupUENQ.

got them back at all. "I thought my life was over," he said.

This was one of the many new fad cyberattacks to hit the market. Hackers would hijack popular YouTube channels to access and trick their audiences into signing up for cryptocurrency schemes.

The hackers were brazen. They deleted all of Drew's videos and changed his channel's name to *Let Us Stream or We Will Delete Your Channel* while streaming their scam.

Drew's future was up in the air. Out of nowhere, everything he built was on the line. "Help! I've been hacked," Drew pleaded to his Instagram followers. Drew's audience mobilized. They flooded YouTube and Twitter with messages and flagged his account to draw attention to the hack.

Drew was lucky. His cries for help worked. He soon got in contact with YouTube's staff. After a few days of back and forth, he was able to get his account back and avert disaster.

Risk = Damage x Existence x Exposure

DAMAGE: WHAT'S AT STAKE?

Let me get something out of the way. I am not a cybersecurity expert. Nobody should hire me to be their cybersecurity expert. What follows comes from my research and talks with much smarter cybersecurity-minded friends. Consider this chapter a brief acceleration along my journey from vulnerable total idiot to less-vulnerable semi-idiot.

Now back to the show.

You've seen the "Big company/celebrity/government agency/utility company/school system gets hacked" headlines. Usually it's some mass data leak or scheme where hackers hold systems hostage in exchange for huge ransoms.

You know cybersecurity is a problem. What isn't obvious is how to think about cybersecurity, how big of a problem it is, why you should care, and what you can do about it. Think about regular security. You live in a home with valuable stuff. Villains want that stuff so they can make money. They can enter your home through the same doors and windows you can. Cybersecurity is kind of like that. You have valuable stuff like money, data, and followers stored in digital places. Cyber villains want it so they can make money.

That's where the similarities end. In regular security there's a small number of doors and windows to enter your home. In cybersecurity there are hundreds and maybe even thousands. It is more like guarding a royal palace than a house.

In regular security the number of villains is mostly limited to bad people who live nearby. You're probably not getting robbed by somebody who lives a thousand miles away. Cybercrime has no geographic barrier. You can be hacked from anywhere in the world.

Most real-world "hacking tools" aren't very complex. You can smash a window with a baseball bat or hold somebody up at gunpoint. In the cyber world, tools and strategies range from the simple, like tricking an old lady to give up her bank information, to the complex, as with software understandable only by sophisticated tech nerds.

There are too many types of cyberattacks to list. However, it's important to get a taste of what exists. The tip of the cyber-fuckery iceberg includes password attacks, spyware, malware, man-in-the-middle attacks, birthday attacks, distributed denial of service (DDOS) attacks, social engineering schemes, phishing, ransomware, trojan horses, SQL injections, and DNS spoofing. If you want to give yourself nightmares, look up the Pegasus software that was used to hack into the phones of people like Jeff Bezos and political dissidents like Jamal Khashoggi.

I won't pretend to know how they all work, but I can describe what's at stake. Everything that powers your business—money, trade secrets, audiences, followers, tax information, financials, legal contracts, marketing content, email accounts, process knowledge, your customers' and clients' information, and even your identity—is on the line.

Yet...

There's a little part of you that knows it's a problem...but not for you.

Why would anybody attack little ol' me? I'm just a small entrepreneur doing small business things. Nothing to see here! Besides, I'm not some naïve grandmother falling for silly schemes.

It's flawed logic impaired by the fact that nobody writes headlines about small businesses getting hacked. You have to dig deep on the internet to find people telling their own stories.

Another YouTuber, Niko Velikov, runs a digital marketing agency. He explains in a video how his Facebook advertising account got hacked shortly after he was tricked into downloading a seemingly legitimate Google Chrome browser extension. The hackers bypassed his two-factor authentication protocols, kicked him out of his own accounts, and began spending thousands of dollars per day promoting their own scam products. Niko had to tell all his clients to cancel their credit cards that were tied to their respective advertising accounts. It took a long time for Niko to recover his agency's accounts, which were critical to managing his business. However, by coordinating with Facebook's fraud department, he was eventually able to get the money lost in the hack returned.[4]

Oscar Gil, who owns an auto detailing business, described his hacking story on a podcast. "I went to my website, where 80 percent of my leads came from, only to find it being redirected to some website selling dick pills." He later learned hackers exploited a vulnerability on his website's hosting platform to insert a virus. His hosting platform had terrible customer service, so he wound up paying some third-party company $600 to get it resolved. Since then, he's switched to a more secure hosting platform and hasn't had any problems.[5]

But for most people, their stories go dark. They get hacked, feel dumb, and never tell anybody about it. This narrative blindness creates a false sense of security that drops cybersecurity far down the list of priorities. You don't think it's a big enough threat for you to divert your attention away from everything else you're doing.

That makes you an easy target. Realizing how big the problem is should be a wakeup call. Current figures estimate the global cybercrime industry to be in the *trillions* of dollars—bigger than the economies of most countries. With technology evolving faster than people's understanding, there's no sign of this slowing down.

You can do something about it now. Or you can find out the hard way like Drew did and watch as somebody destroys everything you've built from the inside out.

EXISTENCE: WHAT RISKS EXIST?

Anything that stores data and money can be compromised. These include the hundreds of innocuous "I totally forgot I made those accounts" you're not thinking of, like hotels you've booked, stores you've shopped at, websites you've bought concert tickets from, and free-trial services you've signed up for.

It's everything in your personal life: your laptop, your laptop's operating system, cloud storage drives, downloaded software, web browsers, plug-ins, phone apps, Wi-Fi connections, text messaging platforms, and emails. It's everything critical to running your business: your website, bank accounts, payment processors, credit cards, e-commerce accounts, social media pages, marketing channels, accounting and invoicing software, and sales systems. Every single one is a unique access point.

However, the most vulnerable access points aren't technological; they're people. It's people inside your business who get tricked into giving up critical information, clicking sketchy links, downloading virus-ridden software, stealing internal company data, and creating openings for hackers to exploit.

EXPOSURE: HOW VULNERABLE ARE YOU?

My overly simplified look at cyber risk looks at ease and the number of access points. The more access points (people and technology), the more windows there are into your business. The easier it is to open those windows, the more likely they will be hacked.

This starts with passwords. The simple test is to think about how many passwords you know off the top of your head. The more you remember, the easier they are, and the more vulnerable they are to attack. Complex passwords are hard to memorize. The more they look like nonsense keyboard salad, like 93!@sv@NDX, the more secure they are.

Go to your internet's browser, and do a quick password check. Before you run it, guess how many accounts you have. Then once you run it, compare that with how many accounts you actually have.

Passwords are only the beginning. Accounts that only require password logins are considered single-factor authorization. Accounts with more barriers are harder to hack than those with fewer barriers. You've seen this when an account texts or emails you a code to log in. This is multifactor authentication. The more multifactor accounts you have, the better.

Here's my idiot-friendly "how worried should I be" cybersecurity matrix:

Fewer Entry Points + **Easy Access:** *Uhhhh, I don't like this.*

Fewer Entry Points + **Difficult Access:** *Yay!*

More Entry Points + **Difficult Access:** *Eh, okay I guess.*

More Entry Points + **Easy Access:** *Oh, fuck.*

CHOOSING CYBERSECURITY RISK

Reality Check: Total cybersecurity is impossible. Guarding your house with a fence, camera, scary dog, and gun will help you against ordinary criminals but not against an army. Same goes for cybersecurity. You can decrease the odds and consequences of cyberattacks, but as long as you use technology, you will never be completely hack-proof. The wrong people with the right resources, sophistication, and patience will always find new exploits.

That being said, there's a lot you can do right now to make yourself less vulnerable. But there is a caveat. Security requires trade-offs. Many of these protocols will slow you down. The point isn't to Fort Knox yourself to where it takes an hour to get started each day.

Cybersecurity Tips

Below are some specific tips and tools that have been recommended to me by smarter people. By the time you read this, those tools might not exist, or there might be better alternatives. Do your own research. You can knock out most of these steps in a few hours.

Don't Click Dirty Links

The internet is filled with shady links to shady places that want to infect your computer with viruses. Always double- and triple-check before you download anything from anywhere. Most ransomware comes from downloading sketchy files sent in email phishing schemes.

Keep Software Updated

Cybercrime is a never-ending cat-and-mouse game between hackers and patchers. Hackers exploit software bugs. Patchers fix bugs and send repairs to users in the form of software updates. Rinse and repeat. The problem is when you don't update your software and leave yourself exposed to old exploits. Keep software updated to plug open holes.

Back Up Regularly

The great thing about data is that you can copy it. Copy and store important data in servers or hard drives disconnected from the internet. That way you can recover your data if it ever gets deleted or hijacked.

Use Antivirus Software

Use antivirus software to block sketchy shit from getting onto your computer.

Reduce Your Digital Footprint

All accounts are access points that contain private information. The fewer accounts with less information, the less there is to attack. Use data ownership and data management software to scrub your information off the internet. Unroll.me helps you mass unsubscribe from unwanted emails. The tool mine at saymine.com is something

I've used to get companies to remove my information from their databases.

Do Routine Password Checks

Data gets compromised in big leaks. Use tools like Google Chrome's password checker or Aura to see which passwords need to be changed.

Scramble Passwords

Use password vaults to generate and store scrambled passwords. No accounts should have simple or the same passwords.

Use Multifactor Authentication

Use multifactor authentication on all critical accounts. Text message–based codes are the most common, but people have figured out how to bypass them. There are plenty of software- and hardware-based authentication tools that are more secure, cheap, and easy to use.

Remember Need-to-Access Protocols

The fewer accounts people have access to, the fewer accounts will be compromised in a breach. Minimize people's access to what they need. Nothing more. Your video editor shouldn't have access to your book-keeping software. Your social media manager shouldn't have access to your company's legal documents.

Keep Up with the Times

Hackers are always finding new exploits. You can find out yourself the hard way, or you can find stories where others talk about how they've been hacked. YouTuber RedLine and Instagram cloning schemes are some popular ones right now.

Remember, cybersecurity is primarily a people problem. Like at a restaurant, it's not good enough if the head chef washes their hands if nobody else does. It only takes one dirty-handed cook to poison the food. You and everyone inside your business need to use basic cyber-security hygiene.

CYBERSECURITY OPPORTUNITY

Cybersecurity is the only risk in this book I see as purely defensive. The opportunity is to quickly and cheaply buy yourself the relief that comes with making your business more secure.

TACO STREET AND CYBERSECURITY RISK

I almost didn't write this chapter. I fell for the "I'm too small to worry about" fallacy. I was too busy working on other stuff. After some big data-leak story, I did a password check on my Google security page. I assumed I had two hundred accounts at most.

Nope. I had over seven hundred. Most were accounts I had accumulated over the years since college. Many had the exact same or slight variations of the same password. Worse, the security check I ran showed dozens of passwords had been compromised in data leaks. That meant my emails, phone numbers, passwords, and who knows what else was floating somewhere out there waiting to be used against me.

I freaked out. I found some long podcasts and got to work.[6] I spent days deleting hundreds of accounts and creating new scrambled passwords for old ones. I enabled multifactor authentication on everything I could.

I copied core business data onto backup drives, removed folder access from old freelancers, and unsubscribed from thousands of emails. I installed antivirus software and stopped ignoring software update notifications. For my team, I made sure everyone had access to what they needed and nothing more. This wasn't hard to do since everyone's role is so specialized.

The extra security hurdles make working a little slower, but it's worth it. I know I'm not totally secure. I know there are holes, exploits, and vulnerabilities I haven't even thought of. But I do feel better knowing that whoever wants my shit will have to work a lot harder to get it.

KEY TAKEAWAYS

· Don't ignore cybersecurity. Being a small business doesn't mean you're not a target.

· You can secure your business now the easy way or find out the hard way later.

· Cybersecurity is primarily a people problem, not a technology problem.

· Apply basic cybersecurity protocols like password management

---

6 Dan Carlin's *Hardcore History*, obviously.

and multifactor authentication.

· Accept that security measures will slow you down but will also make it harder for anyone to attack you.

CHAPTER 19

LEGAL RISK

Shaun was rebuilding the media production company he'd nearly lost when the pandemic broke out. One day he landed a big client. "It was a serious client with a big budget, and somebody I was super excited to work with," Shaun explained. "I was doing backflips I was so happy. We went all out. I found this beautiful home in Los Angeles to rent for a video shoot. It was expensive but perfect. I dropped $7,000 for three days.

"At the house I met Donna, the owner. We had a great working relationship. She was so nice and welcoming. I brought her kids doughnuts, and even tea up to her room once. We were in communication the whole time. The shoot went great. At the end I sent Donna a video walkthrough to make sure everything was all right. We wrapped up and went off on our way to work on the next phase of the project. Weeks later, I got a message on the platform I found Donna's house on."

Dear Shaun,
You broke my house rules, Shaun, you fucking fuck. You owe me $5,000!
Pay me or else.
—Donna

These weren't the exact words, but they might as well have been. Out of nowhere, sweet, friendly, Thanks-For-The-Donuts Donna morphed into Donna the Devil.

Shaun was stunned. "Donna points me to the fine print. She used like twenty spaces to hide the fine print down at the bottom of the listing: 'No more than five people are allowed at the house at any given time.

Extra guests will result in a fine of $1,000 per guest per day,' or some shit like that.

"We didn't throw a party or anything. Strictly speaking, we did have more than five people at some times during the shoot, but it was mostly people coming in and out real quick. So technically, we did break the rules.

"Donna could have brought up any issues, you know, when we were there at the house. She was there! She saw what we were doing. She could have brought anything up. But she didn't. Instead she sends me this—not through text, mind you, but through the platform.

"I went through the complaint. There were pictures and videos of us at the house. This was fucking illegal in California! You can't just film people like that without their consent."

At this moment Shaun realized what was going on. The fine print, the secret filming, the fake hospitality. "It was a trap. Donna knew exactly what she was doing the whole time," Shaun fumed.

Shaun called her out. "This is a greed play! You and I both know what you're doing here. Just because I rented your house doesn't mean I'm some big-money baller. I'm a small business owner just like you, Donna."

"Here's my Venmo. I'll settle for $4,000," Donna responded. She didn't even try to argue.

Shaun blew up. "Fuck you. Sue me."

So she did. Donna took Shaun to court.

"It seemed so clear what was going on. What Donna did was illegal.

My best friend is a lawyer, and I didn't even bother consulting her. I figured I'd handle the case myself. We went to court, and I fucking lost. Donna illegally filming us didn't even matter."

That wasn't the end.

"Donna sued me *again* for an additional $12,000! She claimed the emotional distress was so bad she had to leave work for a week and spend money on childcare, therapy, and all this bullshit."

Donna won again. Shaun had to pay all of it. It was most of the money he was set to make from the entire project. "I spent a year on this project basically for free," Shaun lamented.

Money wasn't the only thing Shaun lost. This debacle was only the tip of Shaun's shitshow iceberg. "I had so many projects to track, clients to deal with, employees going missing, and other lawsuits to fight. It was too much. I couldn't handle it anymore. I shrunk things down and nearly shut it down entirely."

Looking back, Shaun reflected, "Be careful about what you ask for. I told Donna to sue me, and she did."

Risk = Damage x Existence x Exposure

DAMAGE: WHAT'S AT STAKE?

Allow me to sip my own Risk Kool-Aid and declare that I am not a lawyer. This is not legal advice. Get legal advice from an actual lawyer. As with Chapter 18, the best I can do is guide you from vulnerable idiot to less-vulnerable semi-idiot.

The legal system is critical for a functioning civil society. It resolves disputes and serves justice. It's a lot better than war. We're fortunate to have it. Unfortunately, people can use it to fuck you. This is **legal risk**. The legal world will introduce you to slow-moving bureaucracies and the darkness of what people are capable of.

It's a common story. One day it's business as usual. Life is great. The next a spooky letter comes in written in a mysterious language called legalese. It's like English. You can read the words, but you can't understand any of it. Here's what it will sound like:

Dear Nazi Pond Scum,
You did an awful, terrible thing to my poor, helpless client. Give us your soul RIGHT NOW or we will ruin your life and take everything.
—From the Law Offices of Jerkoff, Jerkoff and McGill

Welcome to your first legal battle. Odds are your response will resemble the people I researched.

It was the first time I vomited from stress.

It was horrifying.

My butthole clamped up. I got sick to my stomach.

It was unlike anything else I've ever experienced.

I was insanely nervous.

I didn't have the resources to fight a lawsuit.

And that's just the beginning. There are a few ways legal battles can go. You can sort things out before they escalate. You can back down and take the loss. Like Shaun, you can puff your chest, rattle your saber, and roar into battle, screaming, "I'll see you in court!"

Spoiler alert: Most conflicts don't make it to court.

Once the conflict begins, you'll learn a few things.

Lawsuits are expensive. Merely defending yourself, even against baseless claims, can cost absurd amounts of money.

Lawsuits take time. They involve lengthy filings, depositions, hearings, motions, discovery, evaluations, judgments, appeals, more appeals, and rulings. Pair that with underfunded and overworked judicial bureaucracies, and you have a recipe for long, drawn-out conflicts.

Lawsuits are emotionally draining. They can ruin relationships, expose you to people's worst qualities, and plunge you into a dark cloud of prolonged uncertainty.

Lawsuits distract you from your business. The time you spend fighting legal battles could be spent on your business or living a happy life.

Worst of all, lawsuits expose the darkness inside people. This was the lesson Shaun learned the hard way. "Donna seemed like such a nice person. I trusted her. To realize she was plotting against me the entire time fucked me up."

Then there are the resolutions. In a just world, you'll emerge victorious and win a fat reward while your evil foe is cast off into the depths of hell. In reality, it often doesn't matter who's right, wrong, good, or bad, but who has more money, time, patience, and raw vindictive cynicism.

In the legal world, you can lose even if you win. You can "win" only to find out you can't collect anything from your opponent because they don't have any money to collect. You can "win" and still find yourself financially ruined from the battle. Even if you're "right," you can still lose due to legal or bureaucratic technicalities. Only lawyers are the true winners at the end of the day.

EXISTENCE: WHERE DO LAWSUITS COME FROM?

Anyone can sue you at any time for any reason. It's best to understand who you're most likely to deal with and why. Here are a few possibilities.

Bullies

Bullies are people or companies with lots of money who use the legal system to attack potential threats. They typically target people they assume can't afford to defend themselves.

Note: For this following story, I anonymized the names and details in order to respect the nondisclosure agreement signed by both parties.

One such bully targeted my friend Lauren, who ran a cute lunch spot named Jolly Table. After raising millions in private equity, another Austin restaurant named Douche Table filed a trademark lawsuit over use of the word *Table*. Lauren didn't have millions of dollars like the company behind Douche Table did. She was vulnerable.

"My intention is to do everything I can to keep them from bullying me out of business with their ability to outspend me," Lauren told a local reporter. Fortunately, Douche Table's plan backfired. Once word of the lawsuit got out, the public's reaction was fierce and swift. People saw through this clear bullying tactic. A judge threw out the case, and the two parties settled out of court.

It's never a good idea to brush off a bully's legal threat. However, like most schoolyard bullies, they are often more bark than bite.

Trolls

Trolls are bottom-feeding pond scum. Trolls rarely run actual businesses.

Instead, they're holding companies for vague patents, copyrights, and trademarks. Their entire "business model" is suing people who "infringe" on their intellectual property. The strategy is to get people to pay extortionary settlement fees or risk financial ruin from defending themselves.

Often their claims are absurd. One famous example was when a notorious patent troll, Personal Audio LLC, sued podcaster Adam Corolla, claiming they owned the copyrights for "systems for disseminating media content." Basically, Personal Audio claimed it owned the patent to all podcasting. Despite raising over half a million dollars, Adam still spent hundreds of thousands of his own dollars on defense.

"The lawyers billed me $86,000 for trying (and failing) to get the venue changed from Lubbock, Texas, to Hollywood, California," Adam ranted on a podcast. Technically, Adam "won" the case and didn't pay Personal Audio a dime. In reality, only the lawyers won.

People Close to You

It's far more likely you'll battle people you do business with. These include employees, clients, landlords, freelancers, vendors, suppliers, contractors, and, most importantly, business partners. These can be the most devastating. Rather than battling evil trolls and bullies, you're battling people you have intimate relationships with. Those relationships become casualties of war. This was part of Brad Larsen's experience with Float Temple (see Chapter 5). The good friends he became business partners with became former friends and legal rivals.

You

Don't assume you'll always be on defense. You may have to go on offense to enforce contracts or protect your intellectual property from shady assholes.

EXPOSURE: HOW LIKELY WILL YOU HAVE LEGAL PROBLEMS?

It's hard to predict how and when you'll get into a lawsuit. Consider the following categories as they relate to your business.

Industry

Different industries have different legal risks. You're more likely to get involved in legal battles if you deal with complex, high-stakes transactions like commercial real estate than if you sell lemonade at a farmers' market.

Transaction Volume

The more people you work with and the more contracts you sign, the more likely one of those transactions will end up in a dispute.

Written versus Verbal Agreements

All agreements are points of conflict. The more verbal agreements you rely on, the more room there is for misunderstandings and conflict.

Attention

The more attention you get, the bigger target you'll be for jealous rivals and trolls.

Sharkiness

Sharkiness is a vague measurement of how much people like conflict. The sharkier somebody is, the more likely they'll dive into conflict. The more sharky people you deal with, the more likely you'll find yourself in battle.

"Those influential thought leaders, supposedly enlightened spiritual coaches, and wise entrepreneurial masters you hear on podcasts? Fucking cutthroat sharks everywhere. So many of them go straight to lawsuits at the first sign of conflict," Shaun reflected after finding out the hard way too many times.

LEGAL OPPORTUNITIES

Getting your legal bases checked is an opportunity to turn the inevitable lawsuit from a frantic panic story into a calm, cool, and collected "Let's see what my lawyer says about this" story. It's an opportunity to resolve small conflicts today before they firestorm into wars later.

But the law can be about offense too. I'll assume you're not a psychopathic troll using the legal system to fuck people for profit. It pays to know the rules, or at least know somebody else who knows the rules. The legal system is filled with rules, workarounds, and loopholes that can unlock new ways to do business or save money. For example, nothing is easier money than having the right accountants and lawyers find ways for you to save money on taxes. This will save you tons of money in the long run.

CHOOSING LEGAL RISK

Let me again point out that I'm not an attorney. None of this is legal advice. Assume everything here has many layers of nuance. This is nothing more than an idiot-level primer. Get an actual attorney.

Limit Personal Liability

In a sole proprietorship (a.k.a. operating as an individual with no legal entity), you're personally liable when things go wrong. Lawsuits can end with you losing everything.

Corporate structures, like limited liability corporations (LLCs) were specifically created to limit your personal liabilities. That way if your business gets sued, it's harder to lose your personal stuff. There are many structures to choose from that work differently. Work with a professional to help you pick the right one.

Study Your Industry

You're not the first one in your industry. You wouldn't be the first one to get sued in your industry. Study lawsuits businesses like yours have fought. Odds are if you keep seeing the same thing over and over, you'll have those same problems down the road.

Get Insurance

Some industry-specific insurance policies help guard against losses in lawsuits. Research what options are available in your industry to see what's right for you.

Find the Right Attorney

A divorce attorney won't help you with intellectual property. A tax attorney won't help you with real estate law. Nobody will be better equipped to help you prevent and resolve legal problems than a lawyer who's worked with businesses like yours.

Don't Swim with Sharks

Most conflicts are with those close to you. Few things will insulate you better against stupid lawsuits than avoiding business with the wrong people.

Communicate. Communicate. Communicate.

Most conflicts come when people disagree. Never rely on verbal agreements. It's tempting to skip the awkward step of formalizing written contracts, especially with close friends and family. *You know each other! You trust each other! You wouldn't try to screw each other right...right??*

Wrong. Sure, some people make it work, but it's a terrible long-term strategy. It's extremely easy to disagree over seemingly simple things. Fifty-fifty may mean one thing to you and something completely different to your partner. Have uncomfortable conversations now or pay the price later.

Get It in Writing

Use attorney-drafted contracts to clarify roles, ownership structures, equity splits, expectations, profit sharing, contingencies, and dispute resolution. Update agreements as circumstances change. When conflict arises, you can refer to the agreement.

In the same breath, keep all written communication. If you can't prove somebody said something in writing, you'll get stuck in hard-to-resolve he-said-she-said battles. Written communication will serve as legal ammunition if it ever comes down to it.

This was one of Brad's mistakes in dealing with his business partners. He relied on handshake agreements to temporarily resolve conflicts. Those partners would eventually ignore those agreements as if they never happened.

Resolve Quick

Don't get swept up in the emotions lawsuits invariably trigger and allow battles to become wars. Conflicts become more stressful and expensive the longer they drag on. This is why you have a lawyer. They can better detect whether you're dealing with an all-bark-no-bite bully or a serious threat.

A caveat: Most lawyers get paid by the hour. The more they work, the more they get paid. It's their natural incentive to prolong conflicts. This is why you need a good lawyer who has your best interest in mind.

WAYS TO RESOLVE CONFLICTS

Here are some ways to resolve conflicts, from cheap and easy, to complex and expensive.

Direct Communication: Talk to people directly to see if you can find a resolution before getting lawyers involved.

Mediation: Mediation is where you bring your case to a neutral judge who recommends a legally nonbinding resolution.

Arbitration: Arbitration is like mediation, but where the resolutions of the arbitrator (also known as a private judge) are binding.

Litigation: Litigation is war. It's expensive, lengthy, and draining, and it should be treated as the absolute last resort.

TACO STREET AND LEGAL RISK

My first legal battle came long before Taco Street. I was a new real estate agent in Miami, selling my first client's home. I put their house on the market and began collecting offers. One sketchy agent came by and said they'd send an offer later that night. The sketchy-agent-offer came in well below the others, so I brushed it off.

Later, I got a flurry of emails from the agent and her client demanding I sell them the house. They claimed I said a bunch of shit I never said. The next day I got a spooky letter written in legalese. I'll paraphrase:

Dear Alexander,
Fuck you, you fucking fuck. You fucked me. Now I'm going to fuck you times a million unless you sell me the house.
—From the Law Offices or Jerkoff, Jerkoff and McGill

I freaked out. I had never been threatened like that before. Was I going to lose my license? My client? Was my career over? Luckily I had an ace up my sleeve: Dad. With nearly forty years as an attorney, he's no stranger to legal fuckery. It took one whiff of the letter to smell a rat.

"Alexander," he sighed, "you have no idea how many times I've seen this before." Dad knows a bully when he sees one. It turns out this is super common. Real estate (especially in South Florida) is rife with hyper-sharky pond-scum "investors" who use legal threats to bully people into getting what they want.

Despite having done nothing wrong, I spent the next few months stressed out and worried about my future. I wound up losing my clients, but I eventually won the lawsuit and moved on with my life. I was grateful in retrospect. I saw the legal system in action and came out on the other side unscathed.

This debacle was a big reason I stuck to apartment locating. Deals are simple and lower consequence, and they don't involve me touching complicated contracts. The only lawsuits I've heard of in apartment locating involved outright fraud or invoice collections disputes.

I almost had to sue a former partner when he tried screwing me out of money he owed. My attorney/sister sent him a spooky letter reminding him of the contract he signed:

Dear Fucking Guy,
I see you being a slimy little fuck-weasel. It's not working. You signed a contract. Pay now or else we're going to fuck you.
—From the Law Offices of Big Sister You Don't Want to Fuck With and Associates

He paid.

With Taco Street, my lawyers and accountants have saved me a ton of money using the right corporate structures. One year, for complicated regulatory reasons, I couldn't use this structure and got hit by a surprise $23,000 tax bill, which sucked. Otherwise, there isn't much room for conflict inside Taco Street either. I have no business partners or employees, only freelancers with simple agreements.

KEY TAKEAWAYS

· The legal system can be one of the most useful or devastating aspects of being an entrepreneur.

· Words are weapons. Use them well or they will be used well against you.

· Never underestimate how destructive legal battles can be, how malicious people can be, and how easy it is for people to interpret things differently.

· Watch who you do business with.

· Get things in writing.

· Hire the right attorney.

· Choose your battles wisely. Don't let battles become wars.

CHAPTER 20

MONEY RISK

And you thought we were done with bananas.

Nope.

In the Replacement Risk chapter, we looked at how Jesse Cole and the Savannah Bananas stayed profitable during the pandemic by finding new ways to make money. That was part of the story.

But making more money wasn't enough. They had to cut expenses. Timing couldn't have been worse. "We only play in the summer. Our entire business is built on two months of revenue," Jesse said. The pandemic, which started in March, hit right before their only money-making months.

Making things harder, Jesse wasn't willing to let people go. "We're going to try to cut every other cost we can but not cut our people in any way." Plus they had an entire stadium to pay for.

They had some fallbacks. They had cash reserves to hold them over for a while. Emergency government funding helped too. But if they were going to survive, they had to get scrappy. Money wasn't coming in, and reserves were draining fast.

Jesse tells the story on his blog.[7]

---

7 https://findyouryellowtux.com/leading-in-uncertain-times-with-jesse-and-emily-cole/.

"We called for every single discount and deal we could get. We called every single vendor, every single monthly payment from subscriptions, online stuff, utilities, phone bill to everything.

"We talked to everybody and then what happened is every single group worked with us because we've been a great customer over the years. Everyone said, 'We'll waive this payment. We'll waive that. We'll defer this. We'll discount that.' The reality is we still took a seven-figure hit to our business from our top line but we found a way to eek a little bit of profit."

It's important to emphasize what Jesse and his Savannah Bananas pulled off. They stayed *profitable* in a year when their only moneymaking season was cut off.

This next money-risk story is not one I'm happy writing about. Even before I started writing this book, I had been visiting Scribe Media's headquarters in Austin, Texas, for a period spanning five years. The office started small and quaint, with a few tables and conference rooms. Each time I visited, their office grew by taking over the spaces of neighboring businesses. Along the way, *Entrepreneur* magazine awarded Scribe #1 Company Culture in America in their small business category.[8]

To an outsider, these expansions made sense because they were growing like wildfire, with more author clients, employees, and freelancers. As I was completing this book's first draft, I visited Scribe's office to meet with my publishing manager. This visit was the most peculiar. The office space had exploded in size, taking over much of the building they occupied. I felt like I was inside a major technology company. It was a beautiful space, coated with fresh purple paint, a brand-new studio, and hundreds of books by authors who had successfully gone through Scribe's process. I imagined this book would soon be on their shelves.

---

8 https://www.entrepreneur.com/author/jt-mccormick

But what I didn't see threw me off: people. I saw rows and rows of empty chairs, unused computers, and vacant conference rooms. This was odd, but I brushed it off, assuming it was due to some hybrid remote work policy, and continued with my meeting.

Not long after that, I read some disturbing news. Nearly a hundred Scribe employees were laid off without severance. Scribe's award-winning CEO abruptly resigned. A domino of tragedies followed. Freelancers reported being left with work unpaid. More layoffs followed, hollowing out Scribe to a fraction of its former size. Authors (me included) who had already paid Scribe for publishing services were left with unfinished projects.

It turns out the tingling risk senses I'd ignored on my recent visit were a giant red flag. Scribe was spending far more money than was coming in and was on the verge of bankruptcy. They spent an exorbitant amount of money on the office expansion, which came with ballooning rent and salary costs. I drove to their headquarters with the same morbid curiosity that led me to write this book. Everything was the same. The lights were still on. The same books, computers, and trophies of past authors sat as they were before. The only difference were the white papers taped on each window for passersby to see: eviction notices written in dreaded legalese:

Dear Scribe,
All of your shit now belongs to us. Get the fuck out of here.
—From the Law Offices of Jerkoff, Jerkoff and McGill.

Fortunately, as of this writing, Scribe still lives. They were acquired by another company, hired a new CEO, and now have a much smaller office.

Risk = Damage x Existence x Exposure

DAMAGE: WHAT'S AT STAKE?

Beware Domino Risk: It may seem strange to talk about money this late in the game. It's not. Money is obviously important, but it's rarely the direct cause of death. Instead, it's usually the final domino in a long chain of disasters. Eliminating that chain of disasters is what this book has been about so far.

But now it's time to address that final domino: **money risk.** The way people usually talk about money and cash flow is the kind of stuff you see in business school: income statements and balance sheets. Those are useful, but I have nothing to add there. Besides, if you're like most people, those are just jumbles of numbers that don't mean much.

We're going to take a different approach. We won't just look at how much but how and when you make and spend money. Then we'll look at a few things you can do so you don't watch that final domino fall and crush everything you've worked for.

EXISTENCE: WHAT RISKS EXIST?

You run out of money.

EXPOSURE: HOW LIKELY ARE YOU TO RUN OUT OF MONEY?

Let's look at a few reasons you could run out of money.

Knowledge

The less you know about your numbers, the more likely you'll be taken by surprise.

"I wish I knew my numbers," Michael from Geek Tank Games confessed. "I burned through a ton of money for my Kickstarter campaign launches, assuming it would come back to me. Sure, I made a ton of money from the launches, but then I had to pay for artist royalties, advertising costs, affiliates, production runs, platform fees, and taxes. By the end of it, everyone made a lot of money except me."

Margins

Margin is the difference between how much you make and how much you spend. Take two businesses. Both make $100,000 a year. One spends $90,000 while the other spends $50,000. The first is a low-margin business, and the second is a high-margin business.

A low-margin or negative-margin business lives on the brink of disaster. A surprise expense can knock it out. This was Scribe's problem: they were losing money every month. High-margin businesses have a bigger safety net. More margins means more safety.

Cost Flexibility

Costs are fixed or variable. Cost flexibility is how easy it is to change your expenses. Fixed costs are harder to change than variable costs. Fixed costs can be things like debt payments, retail or office space leases, mortgages, and salaries. High-fixed-cost businesses can't handle shocks the same way a high-variable-cost business can.

If revenue from the $100,000 business slumps to $75,000, the fixed-cost business might be able to drop expenses down to $80,000, but the variable-cost business can move to $40,000 and stay profitable. Flexibility is adaptability. Cost flexibility was a big reason the Savannah Bananas stayed profitable during the pandemic.

This was also why Scribe was fucked. Most of their costs were fixed: office rent and payroll expenses. It took mass layoffs and defaulting on their office rent payments for them to attempt to return to profitability.

Timing

Beware Timing Risk: You can get paid before, during, or after transactions.

Imagine your local techno rave. At this rave, the organizers sell tickets and get paid *before* the rave happens. The friendly neighborhood drug dealer gets paid *immediately* when she sells drugs to her fellow ravers. The DJ playing at the rave gets paid *after* they perform. Each has different risks.

The rave organizers have **Whoops I Lost Your Money Risk**. They risk having to give back the ticket money they collected in case they can't throw the rave. Our friendly drug dealer has many risks, but timing isn't one of them. She gets paid on the spot. Nothing to see here. The DJ has **Where's My Fucking Money Risk**. They risk having to chase down the rave organizers for money, taking less than what they expected, waiting longer than they expected, or not getting paid at all.

Both Michael from Geek Tank Games and Scribe had **Whoops I Lost Your Money Risk**. Michael had to fulfill pre-orders from his Kickstarter campaigns. Scribe had to execute on the publishing services their authors had paid them for. Former Scribe members tell me the company was using new-client money to fund old projects. When shit hit the fan, Scribe had no money left to complete many of the projects authors had already paid for.

Density

Beware Concentration Risk: How big transactions are in relation to your total revenue matters. A low-density business is like a taco truck that sells thousands of tacos each year. No taco makes up a high portion of total sales. Losing a few customers isn't a big deal.

A high-density business is like a luxury real estate agent who sells ten houses a year. Every sale is a huge deal. Losing a few clients could be disastrous. High-density businesses are more volatile because their revenue can swing wildly in different directions.

Seasonality

Seasonality is about when you make money throughout the year. Nonseasonal businesses like hair salons, fast-food restaurants, grocery stores, and car repair shops make similar amounts of money throughout the year. Seasonal businesses make most of their money in shorter periods of time. A Halloween store makes money during Halloween. Ski slopes are busy during the winter months. Accounting firms are busiest in spring when taxes get filed.

The more seasonal you are, the more sensitive you are during your peak months. This was one of the Savannah Bananas' biggest vulnerabilities. They make most of their money in two summer months.

Reserves

Reserves are how much money you have as backup. The less you have, the closer you are to disaster. The more you have, the safer you are. Having reserves helped the Bananas stay alive when revenues dried up.

MONEY OPPORTUNITY

Here are some obvious (and nonobvious) benefits to changing the way you make money.

Increase Margins

Low margins are stressful because you're always struggling to keep up. High margins buy you extra peace of mind and money to reinvest in the business.

Make More Money

Sometimes the simplest solutions are the best. Make more money. Sell more stuff. Do more projects. There is no ceiling to how much money you can make as an entrepreneur.

Change How You Get Paid

Getting paid up front is a chance to avoid the stress of chasing money down. Allowing people to pay over time could bring new people in the door. Creating passive income is the holy grail of cash flow, where you can detach money from time, make money while you sleep, and buy yourself security.

Manage Density

The higher your transaction density, the more volatile you are—which can be good and bad. A high-density business like a luxury real estate agent can multiply their money a lot easier than a low-density taco truck can.

Consider Seasonality

Being seasonal is a chance to make most of your money in a short time of the year so you can do whatever you want the rest of the year.

CHOOSING MONEY RISK

Choosing Money Risk is about choosing how you make and spend money. Here are some ways to resolve money problems now so you don't run out later.

Know Where Your Money Goes

It's easy to lose track of money while you're busy doing other stuff. Get good bookkeeping and accounting systems that let you easily see where your money goes.

Increase Margins

Make more money or cut expenses. Here are some options:

Raise Prices

Sometimes the most obvious answer is staring you in the face: raise prices. You may find out you've been undercharging the entire time.

Renegotiate

People don't make money from dead businesses. This is why people you owe money to may be willing to negotiate. This goes for rent, software licenses, suppliers, vendors, contractors, employees, and freelancers. This is a big reason Jesse and the Savannah Bananas managed to stay profitable. As Jesse said, "The lesson is to always ask."

Cut Fatty Expenses

Sometimes it isn't the big expenses but the little ones that pile up in the background. The not-free-anymore trial you don't use anymore, freelancers working excess time, unnecessary subscriptions, ineffective marketing campaigns, and increased insurance premiums could be draining hundreds or thousands of dollars each month without you even realizing it. Regularly look at expense reports and purge anything you don't need.

Increase Flexibility

High fixed costs make it hard to adapt. Find ways to turn fixed costs into variable costs. This could mean things like renegotiating contracts, opting for monthly versus annual subscriptions, shortening the terms of commitments, and working with freelancers over employees. You may spend more money each month, but you'll buy yourself the flexibility in case you need to be agile.

Beware Earned versus Unearned Money

Avoid Whoops I Lost Your Money Risk. Don't do what Scribe did and spend your clients' money before you've done the work to earn it. This is no bueno. Keep unearned money in a separate account if needed. Avoid Where's My Fucking Money Risk. Never assume money is yours until it's in the bank. Expect that people will not pay you, deals will fall through, and sleazy people will screw you. Prioritize today money over tomorrow money. Improve invoice operations. Offer pay-in-full discounts, or take money up front instead of waiting to get paid later. Just make sure you deliver the goods.

Decrease Density

If you make most of your money in a small number of transactions, find lower-value/higher-volume ways to make money.

Boost Reserves

Save more money. I won't give you some arbitrary number of months to have money for. Have more than you think you need. What you think you need factors in what you think can happen. Keeping more than what you think you need factors in things you don't imagine happening.

Get Investors

Investors can be a quick way to get lots of money. However, be careful what you wish for. Investor incentives can complicate your business model and create more long-term problems than solutions.

Phone a Banker

I recently discovered there's an entire industry dedicated to giving businesses money. They're called banks. On top of the usual accounts and credit card stuff, they also offer things like business loans and credit lines.

Business loans are like normal loans. You get a chunk of money and pay it back over time with interest. Credit lines give you access to money, but you don't have to use it if you don't want to. Terms depend on each bank, but generally you pay a monthly or annual fee to access a chunk of money and pay interest on what you use. Even if you never touch it, a credit line can be your last line of defense against running out of cash when things go haywire.

Talk to your banker now to discuss options. It's a common trope in the banking world that the best time to ask for money is when you don't need it. Don't put yourself in a position where you're begging for money because you're broke and desperate.

TACO STREET AND MONEY RISK

Taco Street is a simple business. My accounting team and bookkeeping software make it easy to track where money comes and goes. Here's how the way we make money shapes our money-risk profile.

Margin

Taco Street has always been a high-margin business. We make between 40 and 50 percent more than we spend.

Cost Flexibility

We don't have many fixed costs. We have no office, salaried employees, or heavy equipment. I run Taco Street from a laptop on my kitchen counter. Our expenses are mostly variable. Freelancers work based on how much work there is to do. They work more when it's busy and less when it's not. Everything else is pay-by-the-month software subscriptions and advertising platforms. Agents, when I have them, make money on commission only. If things went haywire, I could cut all those expenses quickly.

Purging

I used to get this queasy step-on-a-scale-after-Thanksgiving feeling about looking at expenses. Part of me was afraid of what I'd find. As long as numbers kept going up, I would ignore the details for months and let things auto-pay. This has proven costly. There have been a few times where I've found some fishy stuff in my expense reports.

The first time I went digging, I found a slew of $25–$50 a month subscription services I wasn't using. I've had to reign in freelancers from clocking in too many hours. Before, I mentioned my sales software ballooning from $25 a month to $500 a month. Another time, I found one of my advertising platforms went from $80 a month to $800 a month. In every case, I nearly puked at how much unnecessary money I was spending each month. These purges have saved a lot of money.

Asking

Some polite pretty-pleases were enough to resolve my above-mentioned software and advertising platform issues. I did freak out when I got hit with that $23,000 surprise tax bill. I thought I had to pay it all at once, which would have been a disaster. My tax attorney (who is also my sister) told me I could ask the IRS to let me pay over time. I gave it a shot and set up a $2,000-per-month payment plan. Later I reduced it to $1,000 a month, which allowed me to keep more money inside the business.

Timing

Where's My Fucking Money Risk is our big money risk. We get paid months after deals close. If I close a deal December 1 and the client moves into their new apartment on January 1, I may not see that check until March, April, May, or even later. That's a problem when we have "today" expenses but "tomorrow" income.

I used to treat money as if it were already in my account when I thought I'd closed a deal. After watching too many deals fall through, I realized I couldn't count my chickens before they hatched. These days I never assume money is mine until it's in the bank.

Seasonality

I make money all year round, but over 70 percent of the year's revenue comes between April and August. Some years it's been great. I'd make a ton of money in summer and travel in fall. In other years, a slow summer has left me scrambling for the rest of the year. I'm always extra sensitive about risk during those moneymaking months.

Density

We close over a hundred transactions each year. No deal makes up more than 2 percent of our total yearly revenue. Unlike a traditional real estate agent who may close a dozen deals a year, losing a handful of clients isn't a big deal for me. This makes things low stress since no single deal can make or break me.

Phone a Banker

I often have more money in outstanding invoices than I do inside the business—sometimes two, three, or even five times the amount. I've worried about running out of inside-the-business money while waiting for invoices to get paid.

I sat down with my banker, discussed options, and got approved for a $30,000 credit line I could use to pay for operations in case invoices took too long to come in. But I got cute, sat on my ass, and let the loan approval expire, assuming I could get it whenever I wanted. Months later, when I actually did want the credit line, I was unable to get approved and had to tap into personal savings instead.

KEY TAKEAWAYS

· Running out of money is rarely the direct cause of death but is often the final domino.

· How and when you make money is just as important as how much money you make.

· Beware low margins. Keep costs flexible.

· Don't be afraid to negotiate and ask for breaks or discounts from the people you do business with.

· Don't treat money as yours until you've done the work *and* you have it in the bank.

· Beware relying on a few high-density transactions to keep your business afloat.

· Purge fatty expenses. Save more than you think you need.

· Protect your big moneymaking seasons.

· Know how you can get outside money from banks and investors.

· Whatever you do, don't run out of cash.

INTERNAL RISK CONCLUSION

Whew! That was a lot!

Let's review.

When it comes to risks you control, you have two jobs: build a business that works, and don't lose control of it.

Your business model is your foundation. Use incentives to make your model work for everyone, or it won't work at all. Whoever controls your marketing controls your business. No business is possible without product-market fit. Even if you have it now, understand if you're a product- or market-oriented person so you can know why you wouldn't have it in the future.

Don't let marketing channels control your business. Diversify and eventually own your access to your market. Never commoditize and allow the market to control your business. Instead, ignore competition and become irreplaceable by doing things others can't or won't do.
Operations are the engine that keeps your business going. Don't overwhelm it with more problems than it can handle. Treat what you don't sell as equally important as what you do sell. People come and go. Do what you can to keep good people, but more importantly, create a Business Cookbook to store your business's knowledge inside rather than outside your business.

You have a technology company whether you realize it or not. Don't take your tools for granted. Being small doesn't shield you from cyberthreats. Take cybersecurity as seriously as you would regular security. The legal system can be used for and against you. Get things in writing. Hire lawyers. Avoid sharky people, and don't let battles become wars.

How you make money is just as important as how much money you make. Keep high margins. Become cost flexible, and cut fatty costs. Know when money is yours and when it isn't. Keep reserve money, and know how to get more of it.

PART 4: THE ULTIMATE RISK

We've been through a lot of shit. We've survived industry pitfalls, market shifts, economic crashes, political turmoil, bad market positioning, marketing disruptions, operational meltdowns, cyberattacks, lawsuits, and cash crunches.

What else can there be? *Surely everything must be over with now!* Nope. This last section is about what all of those risks have in common.

If you don't survive, it isn't because your industry was too hard, costs rose, the economy crashed, interest rates rose, politicians passed mean rules, people didn't buy enough, you had too much "competition," your ad accounts were banned, employees left, tools broke, you fell prey to cyberattacks, you endured a lawsuit, or you ran out of cash.

You didn't survive because:
- You picked the wrong industry.
- You picked the wrong markets.
- You didn't adapt to your environment.
- You chose a broken business model.
- You sold the wrong thing to the wrong people.
- You became replaceable.
- You chose the wrong partners, employees, suppliers, vendors, and tools.
- You left yourself open to cyberattacks and lawsuits.
- You ran out of cash.

Your business died because you let it. It's your job to adapt. It's your job to build something that works. Any other reason is bullshit.

That's why the final section is dedicated to the ultimate risk to your business: you.

A small caveat: Everything in Part 4 applies to you, but can also be applied to the people you work with.

Here we'll look at the following problems.

Competency Risk: Are you capable enough?

Absentee Risk: What happens when you're not working?

Vampire Risk: What happens when you take too much from your business?

Burnout Risk: What happens when your business takes too much from you?

At the end we'll look at the *ultimate* ultimate risk: your business's risk to you.

CHAPTER 21

COMPETENCY RISK

"What are you most afraid of?" somebody asked Tucker Max during a company meeting.

"I'm afraid I'm not the CEO this company needs. I'm afraid I'm not going to be good enough to lead this company where it can go."[9]
The room went silent. Even Tucker was shocked at what he'd just admitted. In 2016, Tucker Max was the CEO of Book in a Box (which eventually rebranded to Scribe Media)—the company he'd founded in 2014. By then they had millions in sales and a small team of eight. They were growing like crazy, which was the problem.

Working with a single client involves complex interplay between high-level professionals and intense attention to detail. Scaling that kind of business is extremely hard, even for seasoned executives. As the company grew, the wheels began falling off. Tucker's team was dropping the ball. Clients were getting pissed, and the business's reputation was suffering.

Tucker had every reason to be confident. He was a multiple *New York Times* bestselling author who sold millions of books. He'd built Scribe's service. He was the most experienced in the room and understood the book industry better than most. Yet deep down, Tucker knew what the problem was: himself.

"I fell into the same trap as a lot of entrepreneurs. Just because we're

---

9 https://www.tuckermax.com/i-fired-myself-as-ceo-why-and-whats-next/.

good at seeing a problem and finding a solution does *not* mean we're good at turning that solution into a big company. Starting something and validating it is totally different than scaling it."

Tucker was great at telling stories, building culture, creating services, and working with people—all valuable things. Tucker was *not* good at things CEOs needed to be good at: hiring, running meetings, leading teams, running operations, and budgeting. He could have tried to learn these things on the fly, but he knew the truth. Remaining CEO risked ruining everything and wasting a giant opportunity. If Scribe was going to survive and thrive as a big company, he had to step down.

That's what he did. Tucker hired JeVon McCormick, who had experience scaling teams, to replace him as CEO. Under JeVon, Scribe would go on to win awards for best place to work, and Jevon himself would go on to win an award for best CEO in Austin.

(This worked...until it didn't. JeVon would eventually resign as CEO after bringing Scribe to the edge of bankruptcy.)

Risk = Damage x Existence x Exposure

DAMAGE: WHAT'S AT STAKE?

Einstein was an idiot. I'll say it again for dramatic effect. Einstein. Was. An. Idiot.

Sure, he did some smart sciency stuff. But everything else? Einstein couldn't speak Mandarin, cut hair, play the guitar, kickbox, run a fine-dining French brigade, recite sixteenth-century Japanese poetry, dance ballet, or ski. When you think about it, Einstein was an idiot in more areas than not.

Einstein was *selectively* brilliant, which makes him just like everybody in history—including you. You built a business. You make things people like. You found a way to make money for yourself and the people around you. That makes you smart—really smart. But no matter how smart or capable you are, you'll only ever be so in a tiny number of areas.

Here lies one of the most important conflicts you'll ever face: ego or business. The egomaniac inside you likes titles like *CEO*, *owner*, and *founder*. It likes being in charge and telling people what to do. It likes the attention and praise that comes with success. Ego doesn't like being told what to do, feeling dumb, or admitting mistakes. It obscures reality, presumes future success based on past success, and convinces you that you're smarter than you are.

Michael from Geek Tank Games had to learn about **the ego problem** the hard way. "I made so much fucking money from my Kickstarter campaigns I thought I was King Shit of the Universe. I thought I could shit in a box and people would buy it, so I ran a production run for a hundred thousand tokens before my fourth Kickstarter launch, assuming people would buy it."

They didn't. His fourth and final Kickstarter campaign flopped, and Michael was left with mountains of products he couldn't get rid of. "My ego got to me. After that debacle, I was done with Geek Tank Games," Michael concluded.

To protect itself, your ego will get you in over your head and risk destroying everything in the process. Survival means putting your business ahead of your ego. That means being honest with yourself about your **competency risk**: how capable you are—but more importantly, how capable you're not.

EXISTENCE: WHAT RISKS EXIST?

Anything you do, you can screw up.

EXPOSURE: HOW LIKELY WILL YOU SCREW UP?

That depends on what you do, how complex your business is, and how competent you are. There's little to no risk in doing what you know, like tying your shoes. There's also low risk in the super complex, like taxes or home electrical wiring. Even your inner egomaniac will know to hire a professional instead.

Beware Middle Risk: The stuff in between is the real risk. It's what you think you can do but can't. That's where you fuck up. Complexity depends on things like your industry, business model, company size, product offerings, operations, technology systems, legal agreements, and cash-flow mechanics. The more complicated the stuff you do, the more likely you'll fuck up. At risk of stating the obvious, easy stuff is easier to do than hard stuff. Easier businesses are easier to run than complex businesses.

Then there's how smart you are. The smarter you are, the more stuff you can do. The, uh, less smart you are, the less you can do.

CHOOSING COMPETENCY RISK

You choose what you do and what you don't do. Here are some ways to work with and around your limitations.

Simplify

Nothing will reduce the odds you screw up more than simplifying things. That could be anything from choosing a simpler industry, market, business model, or marketing strategy; simplifying tasks; picking easier technology; drafting simpler contracts; hiring fewer people; selling less stuff; or selling simpler stuff. Simple is safe. Simple is sexy.

Hire Smarter

Hire smarter people. Smarter people are less likely to screw up. That was what Tucker Max tried to do. He replaced himself with somebody he believed could do what he couldn't. With how things eventually played out at Scribe, the lesson is that knowing when you're not the right person for the job is one thing, but hiring a suitable replacement is another.

Get Smarter

The smarter you are, the more complex stuff you can do. Even if you wind up never doing what you're studying for, knowing just a little about a subject will help you better detect bullshitting frauds from real professionals.

Stick to What You Know

There's nothing wrong with sticking to what you're good at. It might just be exactly what your business needs. After hiring the new CEO, Tucker reflected on his new role.

"I focus on things I like and am good at: creating new products, building companies within the Scribe universe, and building relationships with people we can work with. Scribe needed me, just a me who wasn't the CEO."

COMPETENCY OPPORTUNITY

Let's take a look at some upsides to addressing your capabilities.

Smash the Ceiling!

Competency is your ceiling. You can't safely outgrow the combined intelligence of the people inside your business. Think about what opportunities you could unlock with a skilled marketer, videographer, designer, accountant, operations specialist, or even replacement CEO.

Discover Your Brilliance

Underestimating your intelligence is just as easy as overestimating it. All new challenges are opportunities to find out you're smarter than you thought you were.

Get Smarter

Getting smarter has never been easier. You can find books, podcasts, online communities, courses, YouTube videos, and endless content for just about anything.

Become Less Replaceable

Doctors don't go hungry because they do complex things other people can't do. They will always be in demand. Same applies for business. Fewer people can do more complex things. The more complex things you can do, the more money you can make, the less replaceable you will be, and the safer you'll be.

Harness the Global Talent Pool

Hiring smart people has never been easier. Before, you were limited to the people you knew around you. Now you have a global (and cheap) pool of talent to draw from.

Buy Yourself Relief

If nothing else, hiring smarter means buying the relief of doing something right the first time.

TACO STREET AND COMPETENCY RISK

Before Taco Street, I was convinced I was a complete idiot. Sure, I was book smart and had fancy degrees. But years of failed job interviews had me convinced I was too stupid to ever make it in "the real world." I never imagined starting a business. Stumbling onto Taco Street was the best thing that ever happened for my confidence. I learned I was more than capable of building a small business, creating a brand people loved, designing a service people valued, and streamlining sophisticated operations. I learned I could become one of the best in an industry where most people couldn't cut it.

But the truth was that I stuck to the apartment locating niche because it was easy. The transactions are simple and don't require any special knowledge. Other real estate niches—things like sales, investing, and commercial transactions—intimidated me. So I stayed away.

Ease is why I can't ever fully escape replacement risk. Because apartment locating is easy and has a low barrier to entry, there will always be a lot of people coming into the industry.

These days Taco Street is easy to run. My work is simple. My freelancers' work is simple. I hire professionals to do complicated stuff like web development, design, bookkeeping, law, and accounting.

KEY TAKEAWAYS

· Your business lives and dies based on the decisions you make.

· What you don't do is just as important as what you do.

· Choose business over ego. Accept when you're not the right person for the job, and find people who are.

· Be honest about how smart you are, how smart you're not, and how smart you can become.

CHAPTER 22

ABSENTEE RISK

Trout roe with Concord grape and parsnip tofu. Potato truffle ravioli explosion. Translucent pumpkin pie. King crab soup inside a glass crab and cabbage soup inside Russian nesting dolls. Trumpet mushroom foie gras taco. Flaming chocolate cake masquerading as black volcanic rock. Jackson Pollock–inspired dessert. Edible green-apple balloon. Each dish tastefully paired with wines sourced (presumably) from the vineyards of ancient gods.

This is a taste of what my sister Christine and I experienced dining at Alinea. Alinea is one of the world's best restaurants. It's won every important culinary award, including three Michelin stars, which translates to *big fucking deal.*

Alinea is the manifested dream of Chef Grant Achatz. Grant is a master. In five hundred years, people will study him in the same way we study masters like Shakespeare and da Vinci. What Grant created with Alinea isn't a restaurant—it's a transcendent journey of nostalgic delights, whimsical sights, divine tastes, and masterful craft. In short, Alinea is awesome.

The pressure of running an elite restaurant like Alinea is enormous. Every dish on every night has to be perfect. Their reputation and business depend on it. Alinea demands a delicate balance between operational mastery and artistic brilliance.

Grant worked suicidal ninety- to hundred-hour weeks to make it happen.

On a typical day, he would source ingredients, prepare dishes, cook, train, taste, clean, invent new dishes, tinker with old ones, and inspect dishes for imperfections. Nothing escaped Grant's perfectionist gaze. That is until destiny awarded Grant the most ironic disease someone like him could get: Stage IV tongue cancer. Grant had to act immediately or die. The chemotherapy treatments he started with didn't take Grant out of the kitchen but did take away his most important sense: his taste.

This was a problem. The head chef at the best restaurant couldn't taste food. It wasn't just his life or Alinea at stake. Grant's existential identity was on the line. Grant described the anxiety in his memoir *Life on the Line.*

"If I couldn't taste, could I really be a chef?"

Eventually the treatments became more intense. He was too sick to work. For a guy like Grant, not working was inconceivable. This was *his* restaurant. This was *his* dream. He was *the* guy. How could the best restaurant be the best restaurant if the guy who made it the best restaurant wasn't there? Grant had no choice. He had to rely on his team.

"I knew that the most important aspect of what I did came from within... after all, I had a team of more than twenty highly trained chefs in the kitchen, some of whom had been with me for more than 6 years...I trained their palates to mirror mine. *I basically brainwashed them* into tasting exactly as I did, and now I had no choice but to believe that they had been paying attention," Grant wrote.

Turns out Grant being out of the kitchen was easier than anyone had thought it would be. For months he was out of the picture, but Alinea ran as smooth as ever. Dishes came out perfect, and Alinea's menu kept evolving. It was almost as if he'd never left.

Grant didn't die. The treatment worked, and his cancer went into remission. Despite surviving, Grant was conflicted. If Alinea ran so well without him, what was he good for?

What would he do now?

Risk = Damage x Existence x Exposure

DAMAGE: WHAT'S AT STAKE?

You are the captain of your ship. You give your business life and are responsible for keeping it alive. So what happens when you're not there? It's not the planned vacations we're talking about. **Absentee risk** is about the unexpected emergencies that take you out when you least expect it.

An emergency like Grant's will be like a sudden and dramatic pop quiz. If you're prepared, things will go smoothly, as with Alinea. If not, things will fall apart and compound the personal emergency that took you out in the first place. Without the right preparation, your business may be one accident away from total collapse. But if you play your cards right, getting rid of yourself could be the best thing to ever happen.

EXISTENCE: WHAT RISKS EXIST?

If you work, you can stop working. But absentee risk isn't necessarily about you leaving—it's about the work you do stopping. Say you work with clients, run meetings, host events, and manage social media accounts. When you stop, those tasks stop. What happens then?

EXPOSURE: HOW MUCH DOES YOUR BUSINESS RELY ON YOU?

Your business's reliance on you depends on you and how you've set things up. Let's look at it from a few angles.

Personality

You are somewhere on the outsourcerer–control freak spectrum.

Outsourcerer: You're not lazy; you just have a magical ability to get others to do things for you. Nothing makes you happier than handing off work so you can have more time for yourself. The more of an outsourcerer you are, the more likely your business will be fine without you.

Control Freak: You're the "If you want things done right, do it yourself" type. This may be great for quality, but it makes your business fragile. The more control-freaky you are, the more work you do, and the worse your absence will be.

Grant Achatz wouldn't have become the chef he was if he wasn't a control freak. Building his dream meant controlling everything from recipes, staff, ingredients, menus, suppliers, preparation techniques, presentation, ambiance, to even Alinea's interior design. Only intense, life-threatening, flesh-melting radiation forced Grant to delegate more.

Redundancy

If you're the only one who knows how to do what you do, your absence will be worse. The more people who can do what you can do, the better. Grant was a control freak, but because he'd "brainwashed" his team, they collectively knew how to do what he did. This made his absence easier than anyone expected.

Dog Business versus Cat Business

Your business is cat-like or dog-like. You can't leave dogs alone. They need to be fed, taken out for walks, played with, cuddled, and cuddled some more. You'd be rightfully shamed if you went on vacation and left your dog alone.

Cats are the opposite. They're feral assassins more than capable of fending for themselves. Cats don't give a fuck about you. To a cat, you exist as a part-time food source and passive amusement. A cat-like business will run fine without you.

How do you know which yours is? There's the guess test. How long do you think you can be away from your business before freaking out? The longer you think you can stay away, the more cat-like your business is.

Then there's the know test. How much time can you actually spend away before things start falling apart? Alinea turned out to be much more cat-like than Grant thought.

ABSENTEE OPPORTUNITY

You-proofing your business makes it stronger, reclaims your time, and preserves your energy. Besides, having a well-functioning business that doesn't need you is the holy grail. It's basically passive income. The more time you reclaim, the more time you have for your hobbies, friends, and family. It creates space for you to do genius entrepreneur things.

After surviving cancer, Grant didn't stop doing cool shit. Realizing he wasn't as needed in the kitchen as he thought he was, he doubled down. Grant opened more restaurants and cocktail lounges and published the Alinea cookbook.

Speaking of Alinea's cookbook, I brought up the Business Cookbook before in the People Risk chapter. There I described it as the place you store the recipes it takes to run your business. But your Business Cookbook doesn't merely have to be an internal-operations manual. If used correctly, it can become super effective external-marketing material.

Scribe does this well. They have podcasts, blog posts, a publicly viewable culture manifesto, and even an actual book documenting their entire process called *The Scribe Method*. This stores Scribe's knowledge inside the business and functions as marketing for new clients and recruitment for new employees. Scribe's content demonstrates they know their shit. Who better to hire for a service than the people who wrote the book on that service? If Scribe survives, I suspect they will have their internal cookbook to thank.

CHOOSING ABSENTEE RISK

You control the work your business takes on, the work you do, and the work you hand off. Here's how you can approach you-proofing your business.

Simplify

It's easier to travel with a simple business than a complicated one. Simplify anything that can be simplified.

Outsource and Automate

The more you do, the more you stop doing when you stop working. Outsource, automate, or find replacements who can take over your work.

Do Stress Tests

There are a few ways to stress test your business. A **location stress test** is where you work from somewhere other than where you normally work. Take a work-cation and see if you can be productive somewhere else.

A **time stress test** is when you work less or not at all. Take a vacation and do as little work as possible. See what breaks or slows down and what works just fine. See how long you can stay away from your phone/computer.

Upload Your Brain to Your Business Cookbook

Your brain is your business's most important asset. When you stop working, your business loses its most important resource. Upload as much of your brain as possible into your Business Cookbook in the form of written or video instruction. Remember, your business needs your brain more than it needs your time. Think about this as backup storage. Uploading what you know means your brain is always plugged into your business, whether you're working or not.

If Grant hadn't survived, the Alinea cookbook he created would have let his team recreate and innovate on his vision.

TACO STREET AND ABSENTEE RISK

In retrospect, I had a huge advantage with Taco Street. I was a world traveler before I was an entrepreneur. I designed Taco Street from the ground up so that I could keep traveling. I'm not one of those "remote work from Thailand" types either. When I travel, I *travel*. I disconnect as much as possible. The most I do is send basic texts and emails.

This was why I was so obsessed with outsourcing or automating everything I could. Anything I couldn't imagine doing while traveling had to get off my plate. It's another reason I stuck to apartment locating instead of branching out to other real estate niches. I knew I couldn't relax in Spain if I had to worry about high-stakes real estate transactions. Sticking to a single low-stakes service let me streamline operations to the point where I could travel the world for months without much fuss.

Eventually I figured out the stuff in my head could be great marketing material too. I turned the common conversations I had with clients into blogs and YouTube videos. I made guides on neighborhoods, apartments, restaurants, and anything else I thought my clients would like. Uploading those videos meant my virtualized brain was always plugged into Taco Street, whether my meat-brain was working or not. These videos have become effective lead-generation tools. People watch my videos, read my guides, and become excited clients. By the time they reach me, the "sales" part is already done. Introductory calls that used to take twenty to thirty minutes now only take five to ten.

All this being said, Taco Street is still more dog-like than I want it to be. I can slash variable expenses and book multi-month trips to Europe without it falling apart, but it won't make much money. I'm still the one responsible for making most of Taco Street's money, so I can only stop working for as long as I'm comfortable not making money. This is why I'm still one of Taco Street's biggest vulnerabilities.

KEY TAKEAWAYS

· If the best chef at the best restaurant is replaceable, so are you.

· The more your business relies on you, the more fragile it is.

· Treat yourself as one energy source, but not the only source.

· Stress test your business by taking yourself out of it on purpose before fate does it for you.

· Find alternative energy sources.

· Outsource and automate whatever you can.

· Upload your brain to your business.

· Create contingency plans.

· Make yourself replaceable so you can reclaim your time and energy.

CHAPTER 23

VAMPIRE RISK

"Are you guys talking about Nora?"

My sister and I were walking around an old Miami neighborhood as someone overheard us talking about her grandmother-in-law.

"We are," my sister replied.

"Nora was my landlord!" the passerby said. We weren't surprised. Nora was a lot of people's landlord. Over a few decades, she created an impressive real estate empire, peaking at nearly thirty properties. It seemed like everyone loved, hated, did business with Nora, or lived at one of her houses.

Nora's houses funded a nice lifestyle. She paid for a nice house to raise the kids, private school tuition, big family trips, cheap housing for extended family, emergency medical bills, and eventually retirement. The problem was what wasn't being paid for: maintenance, emergency funds, and even mortgages. Nora would routinely pull money out of the houses to pay for family expenses.

This wasn't a big deal when there was plenty of money to go around. It was a big deal when the housing market crashed in 2008. Housing prices plummeted. Tenants were falling behind on rent or failing to pay altogether. Nora was trapped. Despite owning millions of dollars' worth of real estate, Nora couldn't handle the monthly payments. There was no emergency fund to draw from.

"We almost never had cash lying around," Nora later mused. To avert total catastrophe, Nora had to sell most of her houses or return them to the bank to avoid foreclosure—all at huge losses. Nora managed to hang on to a few houses, but the empire she built over decades nearly vanished in a few short months.

Risk = Damage x Existence x Exposure

DAMAGE: WHAT'S AT STAKE?

Taking money from your business is normal. You need a place to sleep, water to drink, and tacos to eat.

Vampire risk is about what happens when you take too much money from your business. This doesn't happen early on when there isn't enough money to take but later when business takes off.

When your business does better, you do better. Your shitty apartment turns into a nice house. Used cars become new Teslas. Weekend camping trips turn into fancy European vacations. Single-and-thirty turns to married-with-private-school-tuition-kids. This is fine when everything is fine. But when things aren't fine is when the shit hits the fan.

Enter the Vampire's Death Spiral

Business stops being fine, but you still live as if things were fine. That's because it's easier to go up the hedonic treadmill than it is to go back down. Buying a new house or car is easier than selling it. Putting your kids in fancy school is easier than taking them out. Upgrading to first class is easier than returning to economy class.

Nobody likes going back down. It's more tempting to reduce business expenses instead. It's easier to fire employees, freeze marketing budgets, pause new projects, and defer routine maintenance.

To keep your lifestyle, you bleed your business dry and leave it vulnerable. This was Nora's problem. Years of draining money from her empire left it vulnerable. When times got rough, her business wasn't strong enough to weather the storm.

EXISTENCE: WHAT RISKS EXIST?

There exists a chance you take too much money from your business.

EXPOSURE: HOW BLOODTHIRSTY ARE YOU?

That depends on your behavior and lifestyle.

Everyone is somewhere on the vampire-investor spectrum. **Vampires** treat their businesses like cash-flowing piggybanks, whereas **investors** treat theirs like assets. Vampires like to take money out of their businesses, while investors keep it inside. Nora, even though she was literally a real estate investor, was effectively a vampire. She used her properties to fund her lifestyle but didn't keep enough money inside the business to stabilize it when things went south. Andy, the owner of Cool Apartment Agency, also behaved like a vampire. Rather than invest in marketing that could have kept his business alive, he bought a new car and grew his personal real estate portfolio.

Investors see their businesses as assets to put money into. Rather than buy fancy new shit for themselves, investors would rather hire more people, make new products, fix problems, launch new marketing campaigns, and create reserve funds.

Your vampire-y-ness depends on how expensive your life is. The more expensive your life, the more you will take from your business. Being single with a cheap apartment and a used car is different than being married with kids, a vacation home, and private school tuition.

VAMPIRE OPPORTUNITY

Few things will ever give you the same returns as your own business. You're lucky if you can get a 2 percent return on your savings account or 10 percent return in the stock market. Your business has infinite upside. You can multiply your money year after year without anything stopping you. Think about that next time when you're deciding between a sexy new car and reinvesting in your business. Besides, if you don't see your business as an investment, then consider what that says about you as an entrepreneur.

CHOOSING VAMPIRE RISK

You choose how much money you take from your business and how expensive your life is. Take what you need. Leave the rest. Avoid treating your business like a bottomless piggybank. The more you take, the more fragile it will become.

Delay lifestyle creep. Downgrading is harder than upgrading. Make sure your business can safely handle your growing lifestyle before you make any big commitments.

TACO STREET AND VAMPIRE RISK

I had a weird advantage starting off in the industry: I was dead broke. Even after I started making a lot of money, I kept my lifestyle cheap. Sure, I made some upgrades: I bought nicer clothes, ate at nicer restaurants, went on bigger trips, and moved into a nicer apartment. But I still kept costs low. I kept roommates, cooked most of my food at home, and kept my travel expenses reasonable. This let me be hyperaggressive with Taco Street. It let me invest in a professional website, create the Taco Street brand, hire a freelancing team, launch marketing campaigns, and deploy cool technology.

Taco Street was getting amazing returns. Money I was putting into it was multiplying every year. In less than two years, the $1,500 I started with became a six-figure business. But then I got a little vampire-y. I invested less in Taco Street and put more money into stocks, cryptocurrencies, big fancy trips, the occasional three-Michelin-star meal, and eventually a down payment for my first house.

This was great for a while. My investments grew nicely. Then the markets crashed. My investment accounts shrank. Even with roommates, my house was turning out to be much more expensive than I anticipated. Then I got hit by the surprise $23,000 tax bill. This was all happening when business was slowing down. Within months I went from feeling financially secure to worrying about money again. To stabilize, I aggressively cut personal and business expenses and paused all external investments. These days, I'm a lot more careful about what I take from Taco Street.

KEY TAKEAWAYS

· Beware what you take from your business.

· Success is seductive. Be very careful about how you grow your lifestyle as your business becomes more successful.

· Don't fall for the trap. Delay lifestyle creep. Take what you need, but never bleed your business dry.

· Treat your business like an investment, not a piggybank.

CHAPTER 24

BURNOUT RISK

Now take a deep breath in through your nose.

And out through your mouth.

Ahhhhhhhhhh...

Hillarie Rose was in her element: leading a breathwork session for a group of clients. A Swiss Army knife of health and wellness, Hillarie was deep into her yoga and breathwork practices. Sagacity Health, the company she founded, was born from her dream to take her passions to the professional world. She led stress management seminars, coached executives through burnout, taught yoga classes, led breathwork sessions, and sold online courses.

Business was thriving, and so was Hillarie. She was working for herself, making her own money (and lots of it), working her own hours, and doing work she was deeply connected to. Sagacity's success went far beyond her wildest dreams.

But two years into running it, something was off. It wasn't the hours. Hillarie wasn't one of those work-eighty-hours-a-week types. She had time for herself, her hobbies, and her relationships. It was something else.

"I was getting irritated easily—people coming in late to class, the music not working, things not being where they were supposed to be." It was the stuff Hillarie loved that was getting to her. It was physically draining. "I had a body image to maintain. I worked in Miami and New York. I had to look *good*. I kept a super-strict diet and worked out twice a day. That was on top of the classes I taught."

It was emotionally draining too. "In my sessions I had to be *on* all the time. In yoga and breathwork, I had to be totally present. With people, I had to listen—like *really* listen to my clients. I had to hold space for people to talk about their feelings. As an empath, I feel other people's emotions as if they were my own."

The signs were there. "I wasn't listening to my body. When it told me to slow down, I sped up. I was chasing success. I was fulfilling my dreams. I had people to serve and expectations to manage. I couldn't just stop."

Sagacity Health, the business, was thriving. Hillarie, the human behind the business, was falling apart. The same woman training others on how to deal with stress and burnout was herself severely stressed and burning out. "In my classes I was physically going through the motions, but emotionally I was checked out. Even my clients noticed."

Hillarie was physically, emotionally, and spiritually drained. "I could barely sleep. A thousand thoughts would run through my mind at all times. I didn't have time for my emotions. I stopped caring about work. I lost my passion. I wasn't caring about my clients' problems. I wasn't even doing the things I was telling them to do."

Eventually Hillarie's body rebelled. A mysterious illness began shutting her down. "I was in pain all the time and so weak I could barely carry grocery bags. I went to doctors, plant medicine shamans, and tried everything I could, but nobody knew what was going on. How could I be there for my clients if I couldn't be there for myself?"

Hillarie couldn't go on. Two years after building her dream business, Hillarie had to shut down Sagacity Health or risk losing herself in the process.

Risk = Damage x Existence x Exposure

DAMAGE: WHAT'S AT STAKE?

If I have to give one piece of advice to someone who's thinking about starting a business, I tell them this: forget about balance. You're going to work twenty-five hours a day, seven days a week, forever.
—Kevin O' Leary, a.k.a. Mr. Wonderful, entrepreneur, *Shark Tank*

With celebrity entrepreneurs like Kevin saying shit like this, it's no wonder we see the same story over and over. Entrepreneur starts business. Business makes money. Entrepreneur works harder and harder to make more and more money. Entrepreneur neglects health and relationships. Entrepreneur burns out. Business suffers. Life becomes hell. Entrepreneur does ayahuasca in South America and magically discovers they need to take care of themselves.

Well, no shit. How about skipping all that? Working yourself to death is lame. Crashing businesses is no fun. Watching your life fall apart sucks. Tickets to South America are pricey. Ayahuasca tastes icky.

Nobody burns out on purpose. People generally like to live happy, healthy lives. So why is burnout so common? The problem starts when we treat ourselves like businesses instead of humans. This was Hillarie's problem. "I treated myself as a service, not a person. I was afraid of letting people down and ruining my reputation."

The problem with treating yourself like a business is that burnout doesn't show up on expense reports. We don't track time, lost energy, or negative emotions as we would other expenses. We spend it as if it's an infinite resource. Of course, it isn't. You're human. You have only so much to give. Eventually you spend too much until there's nothing more to spend. This is **burnout risk**.

Burnout doesn't just affect your business. It's all-consuming. It affects you, your body, your mental health, and the people around you.

Burnout is insidious because of where the energy comes from. There's the energy that wants to create, build, tinker, solve problems, add value, and help people. But then there's the hidden shadow energy working to fill a void of status, validation, and self-worth.

The shadow's logic is simple: valuable, successful business means valuable, successful person. The more you work, the more successful you become, and the more valuable you are. This works until it doesn't.

EXISTENCE: WHAT RISKS EXIST?

There exists a chance you'll burn out.

There are two types of burnout we'll focus on: the **fast burn** and the **slow burn**.

The fast burn is the one you're probably thinking about. You work a ton over a short period of time and hit a wall. It's like when you're studying for finals, meeting some strict deadline, or coordinating some big new launch. This is what happened to Malcolm from Flowmagin in the Business Model Risk chapter. "I burned out hard core like three times in six months," he remembered.

The fast burn is dramatic, but the drama makes it obvious. If you catch it in time, you can take a break, recharge, and return to normal. If you don't, as Malcolm didn't, then you may sprint straight off the edge of a cliff.

Beware Middle Risk: The slow burn is the dangerous one. Like the frog boiling in water, it happens quietly in the background over a long period of time. It's not dramatic like the fast burn. It doesn't happen over days or weeks but years. Gradually it creeps from the background to the foreground. Good feelings fade while bad ones magnify. Wins stop feeling like wins. Even small losses feel like big ones.

Hillarie's was a slow burn. It wasn't the hours she worked—she rarely worked more than forty a week. It was the slow, repetitive physical and emotional energy slog that drained her from the inside out. By the time she noticed, it was too late.

EXPOSURE: HOW LIKELY WILL YOU BURN OUT?

The more you work, and the more you do stuff you don't like, the sooner you will burn out. That's simple enough.

Then there's your personality. On an oversimplified personality spectrum, you skew toward **extreme** or **balanced**. Balanced people are moderate and take things easy. Extreme people go all out in everything they do.

Hillarie was an extremist. "I went hard with everything. When I diet, I diet hard. I counted my macronutrients. You wouldn't catch me dead eating a tortilla. At my peak I would work out twice a day—on top of teaching regular yoga classes. On weekends I would party hard, get wasted, and do everything to override my senses. It was the same with business. I relentlessly chased success. I would always give clients, students, friends, and partners my all."

BURNOUT OPPORTUNITY

Energy is everything. It's the force that keeps your business alive and brings out the best in life. Taking your energy seriously is an opportunity to give it the attention it deserves. Energy helps your business. Energy is where your creativity and problem-solving abilities come from. The more you have, the more you can bring to the table. More importantly, having energy improves your life. It means more energy for hobbies, health, friends, and family.

CHOOSING BURNOUT RISK

You choose what you do and don't do. Here are some ways to approach burnout.

Prevent Burnout

The best way to resolve burnout is by not burning out in the first place. Problems require energy to solve. The more problems you have to solve, the more energy you have to spend, and the closer to burning out you'll be.

Everything you do about risk is about solving cheap problems before they become expensive problems. *This means everything you do about risk is directly related to protecting your energy and preventing burnout.*

Adapting your business to your environment means you don't have to scramble every time the world changes. Designing a strong business with a working model, streamlined operations, robust marketing strategy, cybersecurity protocols, legal defense, and money management means you're not spending your life force putting out constant fires.

At the end of the day, choosing the right risks is about having less bullshit to deal with.

Do Other Work

Business involves doing stuff you like and stuff you don't like.

Make a two-column list describing work you do in your business. The first lists "shit you like to do." The second lists "shit you don't like to do." Describe how each task makes you feel. Find ways to do less stuff you don't like and more stuff you do like.

Shit I **DON'T** like	Shit I **DO** like
Calling apartment buildings	Working with cool high-budget clients
Invoicing	
Making spreadsheets	Touring people around neighborhoods
Working with crappy clients	
Taxes	Making friends with clients
Bookkeeping	
Lead generation	

Find Other Energy Sources

Your business requires time and energy to run. That doesn't mean it needs *your* time and energy. Treat your time and energy as a source, but not the only source. Preserve your energy by hiring, delegating, and automating things that drain your energy.

Slow the Fuck Down

If more is leading you to disaster, do less. "I didn't have a choice," Hillarie said. "My body was shutting down. I had to slow down. After shutting down Sagacity, all I could focus on was resting and getting better. Recovery was the only thing I became extreme about. For the first time, I really understood what it meant to take care of myself." Over a year after her burnout, Hillarie recovered and is now working a dream job doing what she loves most, but this time she's taking care of herself first.

TACO STREET AND BURNOUT RISK

For better and worse, I don't like working hard. I get stressed and overwhelmed easily. I'm not lazy, but I'm more of a consistent jogger than a sprinter. It's a big reason I spent so much energy outsourcing and automating things I didn't like doing.

For years Taco Street felt like cheating. It was my full-time income but only needed part-time hours to run. I had a good sleep schedule and plenty of time for hobbies, travel, friends, and family. I thought I was immune to burnout.

Nope.

In my third year running Taco Street, I was finishing a busy summer season. I closed a lot of deals and made a lot of money, but something felt off. Wins began feeling empty, but losses felt as painful as ever. In a day I might close a $3,000 deal but lose a $500 deal. Winning the $3,000 deal felt like fulfilling a quota, but losing the $500 deal felt like getting stabbed in the face.

Even though I wasn't working many hours, the repetition was getting to me. Every day was the same. Same phone calls. Same research routine. Same follow-ups. Same tours. It was the same—day after day, week after week, year after year. By the end of that summer, I didn't want to talk to clients, follow up, or tour apartments. I didn't want to do anything. I was sick of it all.

I needed a break. So I went to Hawaii for a two-week reset. I adventured, surfed, ate poke, and rested. It was great. I came home refreshed, hopped back on the saddle, and started cranking out deals again. But the recharge quickly wore off. I was back where I started. The grind was getting to me. I was slowly burning out.

Somewhere I sensed a bigger problem. Burnout wasn't the root cause but the manifestation of something much deeper. Taco Street was fine...but I wasn't.

KEY TAKEAWAYS

· Beware what your business takes from you.

· Your energy is your and your business's most important resource.

· You are a human, not a machine. Your time and energy are precious and finite. Running out of them will ruin you and your business and impact everyone around you.

· Treat everything you do about risk as preserving your energy. Build a business that puts less bullshit on your plate. Redesign your business so it costs less energy to run, or find alternative energy sources.

· Because at the end of the day, risk isn't about your business surviving—it's about you surviving.

CHAPTER 25

RELATIONSHIP RISK

"I can't do this anymore," Bryan Dagle told his wife with tears streaming down his face. Together they were vacationing in Colorado—one of their first as a family. Bryan was beginning a new life. He was recently married, a father to a new son, owner of a new house, and had recently started a new coaching business. This wasn't why Bryan was breaking down. Bryan's relationship with his family was great. It was his relationship with his business that was the problem.

A decade earlier, Bryan quit his job to become an entrepreneur. He started Headset Buddy—a website that sold audio equipment. It soon became a six-figure online business. It was a dream. Bryan was making more money than he ever imagined.

Years into running Headset Buddy, things began to feel off. He would go into the office and grind through the motions. His business began feeling more like the boring office job he'd quit years earlier. It was getting to him. One of his employees even called him out on it. "If you're unhappy, what are you doing here?" Bryan knew she was right. He hired a manager to run things so he could travel.

"It was amazing. I could do whatever I wanted without anyone judging me. Money kept flowing in every month. It was every entrepreneur's dream." This worked until the manager left. The next manager had mixed results. Without Bryan at the helm, business kept shrinking year after year. Time and time again, he had to keep stepping back in to save Headset Buddy. Soon that manager left too. By this point Bryan was checked out. He didn't want to run the business anymore. He had a new idea. This time he hired a new manager who would eventually buy Headset Buddy.

Things were going according to plan...until they weren't. This new manager's personal life fell apart. She neglected work. Orders weren't shipping. Customers were getting pissed. Amazon, where 70 percent of their sales came from, shut down their store. The business Bryan had spent a decade building was on the brink of collapse. This was why Bryan was breaking down. The thing he'd created to free him was becoming a nightmare getting in the way of the new life he was building.

To be the husband, father, and entrepreneur he wanted to be, Headset Buddy had to go—for good. Bryan cut the family vacation short, salvaged the business, and ended his relationship with Headset Buddy by selling it to an old customer.

Ending a long-term relationship, even after it's gone bad, is hard. But what might be harder than that is ending a great relationship.

SUNNY SOCKS

After college, Stephanie Martinez could have gone into management consulting or investment banking or joined a fast-growing startup. She didn't do any of that. Instead, Stephanie wanted to own something that would do more than just make money.

Stephanie met Michelle, the founder of Sunny Socks, whose company sold socks and gave to charities. They quickly become fast friends and cofounders. With Michelle's vision and Stephanie's business talents, they would take Sunny Socks to the next level. Sunny Socks wasn't so much a business but a mission. Early on, they donated one pair of socks to charity for each pair they sold. Eventually they grew into a profit-donation model and developed an employment program to help homeless youths get back on their feet.

For years the mission went well. Sunny Socks grew into a million-dollar business. They've donated 30,000 pairs of socks and $60,000 to charities and have employed over two hundred youths going through homelessness. "A lot of them credit us for getting their lives back together," Stephanie said with pride.

Together, Stephanie and Michelle survived hard times. "During the pandemic Sunny Socks went from days away from bankruptcy to doubling in size." It was one of Stephanie's proudest moments. Strangely, another one of her highlights came when a bigger company began blatantly copying them. "Sure, some people were pissed, but that company was copying us because they couldn't replicate what we were doing," she said.

Nearing the end of a decade working together, Stephanie and Michelle met to discuss Sunny Socks' next decade. For Michelle, Sunny Socks was her life's work. She was in it for the long haul. But Stephanie sensed something else.

Sure, there were ordinary business headaches Stepanie dealt with, but all in all, Stephanie loved Sunny Socks. The money was good, and the work was meaningful. She was creating the impact she'd set out to create. "I actually loved going to work every day," she said. But by then Stephanie had already put nearly a decade of her life into the same project, and she sensed her relationship with Michelle was deteriorating. "We were great friends, but doing business together was becoming a problem." Stephanie needed to grow, but in a different direction. "I've got so many years ahead of me. We're living in the most magical time ever, and I want to be a part of it. I realized I wasn't going to do that here."

"I don't see myself here in five years," Stephanie confessed to Michelle. "I don't think I have more than two left in me."

Michelle didn't take the news well. "If you're not in this for five years, why are you here at all?"

A crack in the relationship became a rift. Stephanie's hypothetical two years became an immediate split. "We could have parted the easy way, but that's not how things went. Lawyers got involved. We were best friends. I went to her wedding, but by the end, only our lawyers were talking to each other. It fucking sucked." Stephanie still feels the sting of leaving something she loved but is excited about starting fresh and building something that aligns with her goals.

Risk = Damage x Existence x Exposure

DAMAGE: WHAT'S AT STAKE?

You are the biggest risk to your business. But this book isn't about your business surviving. It's about you—the entrepreneur inside of you—surviving. The biggest risk to that version of you is your business.

You have a relationship with your business in similar ways you have a relationship with other people. You give your business money, time, and your life's energy. It gives you money, stress, joy, anger, fulfillment, anxiety, comfort, disappointment, and purpose in return. Your relationship with your business is one of the most important relationships in your life. **Relationship risk** is about that relationship becoming one you don't want anymore.

Your relationship with your business can be like any other relationship. It can be great, shitty, or boring. There's the early honeymoon. The thrill of making more money than you ever imagined. The relief of escaping financial anxiety and providing for the people around you. There's the glee of watching your crazy ideas work. There's the conspiratorial "this feels like cheating" feeling of being your own boss, making your own hours, and living on your terms.

But like all relationships, it can sour. A bad relationship gives you less than what you put in. This can look like a lot of things.

It's when your business takes over your life and robs you from your friends and family. You neglect your health. Your inner creator devolves into a petty bullshit-extinguishing firefighter. It's when more clients, customers, and projects give you more stress and anxiety than anything else. It's when your social media persona feels more and more like a fraud. It's when business partners feel more like enemies than allies. It's when the repetitive slog dulls your creative edge. It's when you stop believing in the mission. Eventually the exciting honeymoon fizzles into a passionless coexistence propelled by passive inertia. You cringe at the idea of doing the same thing for years on end. It's when the thing you built to free you becomes a prison of your own making.

The problem is the same problem with romantic relationships: communication. Without it, relationships become dreaded **situationships**.[10] The situationship is an undefined relationship. Without boundaries, it morphs into something nobody wants through passive acceptance rather than by conscious design.

Like a messy divorce, your relationship to your business can be hard to untangle. It's hard to break up with the thing that pays for your house. Unlike a human relationship, you own your business. You have a lot more flexibility and control over the relationship you have with it.

EXISTENCE: WHAT RISKS EXIST?

There exists a chance your relationship with your business becomes one you don't want.

---

10 "Situationship" was coined by Carina Hsieh in "Is the 'Situationship' Ruining Modern Romance?" in *Cosmopolitan* online, May 1, 2017, https://www.cosmopolitan.com/sex-love/a9566889/what-is-a-situationship/.

EXPOSURE: HOW IS YOUR RELATIONSHIP WITH YOUR BUSINESS?

I'll focus on three types of relationships: hyperobsessive, toxic, and boring. Pay attention to which type you relate to the most.

The Hyperobsessive Relationship

You are your business. Your business is you. You obsess over it, live it, and breathe it. You give it everything. In return, it takes everything. It takes your life, costs your health, and robs you from the people you love. These are the hypersuccessful gazillionaires who are "crushing it" and wondering why they're still single or divorced or why their kids won't talk to them. They are successful on the outside but miserable on the inside. This was Hillarie's relationship with her business in the Burnout Risk chapter. She gave her business everything until her business nearly took everything from her.

Here's a thought exercise. Take the first entrepreneur/influencer you like that comes to mind. How would you feel about them and their advice if you found out they were miserable inside? Would you wish for their blessings if you had to take on their curses?

The Toxic Relationship

The toxic relationship is the "can't live with it, can't live without it" relationship. You're tired of it and want to stop, but you need to pay the bills. For years this was Bryan's relationship to his business. He got tired of running it but needed the money it made. Sometimes a manager could run it, but he constantly had to jump back in to keep it from crashing. This wasn't sustainable.

These first two relationships obviously suck, but their obviousness makes them addressable.

The Boring Relationship

Everything seems fine on the surface. Business is going well. The money is good. Life seems fine. But somewhere inside you know something is off. The energy you used to feel isn't there anymore. You don't feel the joys or thrills you used to. The honeymoon is over. Your good-kids-pretty-house-nice-neighborhood relationship with your business has dulled into a passionless coexistence of quiet desperation.

Beware Middle Risk: Boring relationships are the most dangerous relationships. They're the easiest to ignore and the hardest to admit. They're not bad enough to leave but not good enough to love. It's why boring relationships coast on for years on passive momentum until one day you wake up wondering what the fuck you've been doing with your life.

In business you don't care like you used to. You aren't creating or solving new problems. Instead you're coasting. Boredom is death by passive acceptance.

This was the trap that Stephanie was avoiding with Sunny Socks. Her relationship with Sunny Socks wasn't bad, but it wasn't good enough to light her fire. Only after imagining herself doing the same work years into the future did Stephanie realize she was in the wrong relationship.

RELATIONSHIP OPPORTUNITY

The greatest opportunity possible as an entrepreneur is having an amazing relationship with your business. It's the relationship where you get all the money you want, the time to spend how you want, and the boundless energy for the work you love. There's a reason "if you do what you love, you'll never work a day in your life" is such a common trope. The ultimate relationship is where your business is not just some moneymaking machine but the profitable expression of your highest traits.

CHOOSING RELATIONSHIP RISK

The most important thing you control in your business is your relationship with your business. Here are a few ways to approach improving your relationship.

Describe your relationship to your business. How do you feel about your work? How do you feel about your customers, clients, business partners, and anyone else you work with? What, if any, meaning do you find in your work? Can you imagine your current relationship becoming a long-term relationship?

Don't let your relationship with your business become a situationship.

Define the relationship you want. Describe what you want to be doing and what you don't want to be doing. Write out the relationship you want with your customers, clients, audience, business partners, and anybody else who matters. Describe the money you want to make and how you want to spend your time. Describe what you want to feel and what you want to avoid. Describe the role you want your business to have in your life.

Create Boundaries

You are not your business. You are a human who owns a business. Without boundaries, you risk your business taking over your life. If you find yourself drowning inside your work, describe ways you can create more rigid boundaries so it doesn't overtake your life. Maybe that starts with working fewer hours, becoming more selective with the work you do, firing clients, or shrinking the window of time people can communicate with you.

Choose Better Risks

Everything you do about risk is in one way or another about improving your relationship with your business. It's easier to like a business that doesn't pile you with bullshit. Choosing the right risks will give you more good stuff and less bad stuff.

Change the Relationship

Owning your business means choosing your relationship with it. Remember that owning it doesn't necessarily mean running it. This is what Bryan initially did with his business Headset Buddy. Hiring a manager changed his relationship from business *operator* to business *owner*. You choose your role inside your business. Maybe you hate being CEO but love marketing, making products, writing, throwing events, or working with clients. Find a way to focus on what you like.

Maybe the best relationship means less. Take fewer clients and customers. Work fewer hours. Offload more work to employees and freelancers. Shut down the brick-and-mortar retail store. Use technology to get menial stuff off your plate.

Go polyamorous. Start another business. Start other projects. Turn your business into a side gig, hobby, or passion project. Lukas from Good Property Services turned his business into a side gig while he found a full-time job. Zach from Live a Great Story scaled back his business so he could travel the world and go on epic adventures.

Maybe changing means more. Reignite the raw energy that got you here to begin with. Make new products. Solve new problems. Start new projects. Find new things to get excited about.

End the Relationship

A failed relationship is not one that ends, but one that lasts longer than it should.
—Neil Strauss.

Same with a business.

Maybe there is no salvaging the relationship. Like Bryan's relationship with Headset Buddy, your business may become the thing stopping you from going where you want to go. In this case the best relationship with your business may be no relationship at all.

Tucker Max and Zach Obront, Scribe Media's original founders, eventually left the business they founded. "Scribe didn't need me anymore," Tucker later said, "and I didn't want to be there." Tucker had nothing left to give. He left his company so he could build a ranch and spend more time with his family.

Zach wrote, "I started Scribe when I was 24 years old. I barely remember what work was like outside the container of this company. I love so much about the team, the authors, and the mission—and yet, I have a deep sense that now is the time to step back into the exploration and uncertainty of a new chapter."

Sell Your Business

You can't sell your girlfriend or your boyfriend, but you can sell your business. Sell it to someone who values your business more than you do.

Shut It Down

After all this time we've spent trying to keep your business alive, the final irony is that maybe it shouldn't survive. Surviving isn't about your business surviving. It's about you, the creative-problem-solving, mad-genius human behind the business, surviving. And if your business is the thing keeping you from the life you want, then it needs to go.

Michael Kane from Geek Tank Games, the guy with epic Dungeons and Dragons tattoos all over his arms, didn't want to play Dungeons and Dragons anymore. The passion he turned into a business corrupted the passion that led him to do it in the first place. "I was doing so much DnD-related work that I didn't want to do it for fun anymore." Michael shut down Geek Tank Games, but he's back to playing Dungeons and Dragons for fun again.

TACO STREET AND RELATIONSHIP RISK

I'll never forget my first apartment locating check. It was $1,500—the same amount Dad was sending me each month to cover living expenses. "I think I'll be okay this month, Dad," I told him, relieved. What I never could have known was how okay I would be. You can imagine my surprise when that $1,500 check became $10,000 weeks, $40,000 months, and $200,000 years.

What was supposed to be a brief detour on the path to a steady salary wound up changing my life forever. My old shitty apartment became an amazing downtown apartment, which became my own house in my favorite neighborhood. Financial anxiety was a feeling long past. These days, few things seem more absurd to me than the idea of going back into an office.

Taco Street let me breathe easy when the pandemic was tearing the world apart. It taught me more about business than my business degrees ever could. It saved me from a simulated corporate reality and opened the door to life on my terms. It showed me what it was like to own the fruits of my work. It proved I could build a career around the life I wanted rather than settle for the inverse.

Taco Street became a profitable expression of my personality. It was the canvas where I could bring my crazy ideas to life. It was my mirror that taught me about myself, accelerated my personal growth, and gave me the confidence that I could be an entrepreneur.

Sure there were headaches. Clients ghosted me. Deals fell through. Taxes surprised me. I had to fight to get paid on invoices. But overall, the work was good. I liked (most of) my clients, and they genuinely appreciated my work. Some even became great friends. I felt like an overpaid tour guide, helping people discover the city I loved. The best part was the freedom I had to travel, explore hobbies, and spend time with my family whenever I wanted. But more than anything else, Taco Street showed me what it was like to bet on myself and win.

It was a dream.

Until it wasn't.

Somewhere along the way, the Taco Street honeymoon had ended. I had been going through the same motions day after day, month after month, year after year. I was bored, but I didn't realize it right away. Taco Street the business was fine, but I, the entrepreneur, was dying. I wasn't creating or solving new problems. Beyond the routine expenses Taco Street paid for, I stopped caring how much money it made.

Instead I was half-assing work, letting obvious opportunities pass by, ignoring glaring vulnerabilities, and coasting off the energy from days long past. I imagined myself years in the future, doing the same phone calls, same tours, same routine, same same same. *Fuuuuuuuuck no.* It crushed me. I found myself staring at a professional dead end, fearing I would become a prisoner in a cell of my own making.

But along the way I found a surprise blessing. Getting a little meta here, this book changed my relationship with Taco Street.

What had become a tool to maintain my status quo became the financial engine for my life's most important work. The more time I spent writing, the more obsessed I became with this book. Energy that would have gone to Taco Street went here instead. Taco Street became my muse and the guinea pig for the ideas in this book. On top of the money, Taco Street gave me the time and space needed to bring this new thing to life.

I can't break up with Taco Street—at least not yet. I've got a mortgage and too much stuff to pay for. Losing Taco Street's income would be a disaster. I'm still grateful for what Taco Street provides me. I still like meeting new people, the money I'm making, and the free time I have. My situation could be way worse. But the "fuck, am I really still doing this?" feeling is a part of each day now. More and more, it feels like I'm stuck in a boring, borderline codependent relationship.

I'm not even sure if I want to break up with Taco Street. There are still so many opportunities to create value and build wealth, but if I'm going to access those opportunities, I'll have to find a new way to do it.

I don't know where my relationship with Taco Street is going. If and how I solve this relationship problem may be the subject of another book.

KEY TAKEAWAYS

· Your relationship with your business is one of the most important relationships in your life.

· You can choose a bad relationship that makes your life hell, a boring one that drains your energy, or an amazing one that fills you with riches, time, and meaning.

· Describe the relationship you have and the one you want—and what it will take to make it happen.

· If your business must die so you, the entrepreneur, can live, then so be it.

THE ULTIMATE RISK CONCLUSION

You are the ultimate risk and opportunity to your business. Nobody has more influence over it than you. You are responsible if it dies, survives, or thrives. Don't put your ego over your business. Know when you're the right person for the job and when to lean on others.

Practice taking yourself out of your business before life does it for you. Offload work. Automate routine tasks, and upload your brain to your business so that it runs well without you.

Beware what you take from your business. Don't let your lifestyle drain it from the inside. Instead, treat your business like the asset it is. Be careful what your business takes from you. Treat yourself as a human, not a machine. Recognize your energy as your most important resource. Otherwise you and your business will burn down together.

You are the biggest risk to your business, but your business is the biggest risk to you. Your relationship with your business is the most important choice you make as an entrepreneur. At the end of the day, you are more important than your business.

CHAPTER 26

THE FINAL EXAM—GROWTH RISK

By all objective measures, Carlos Concepcion, a.k.a. Dad, is the world's best attorney. Early in his career, he knew he wasn't suited for the big corporate world. Dad is a rebel. He needed to do things his way and live on his own terms. In his early thirties with a mortgage, a wife, and two young kids (this author included), he escaped the corporate jungle to do something few others had the audacity to do: start his own law firm.

At first things were turbulent. His former employer tried (and failed) to sue him. Losing his one and only client could have put him out of business. Later, one of Dad's biggest clients screwed him out of the money he owed and almost bankrupted his firm.

But soon things took off. More cases came in. For the first time, he started making good money. His big bet on himself was paying off. The more cases he did, the stronger his reputation became. Eventually he got a full-length feature in Miami's biggest business publication.

Dad's small firm became a big deal. He traveled the world, flew first class, stayed at the nicest hotels, and rubbed shoulders with the global elite. Small clients became big clients. He worked with multinational corporations, banks, the superrich, and even politicians.

Then the 2008 financial crisis hit. It was the best thing that ever happened. Rich people and companies love suing each other when shit hits the fan. Resolving these battles is what Dad's firm specialized in.

Big cases came in left and right. They were raking in more money than they knew what to do with. More casework meant more employees, lawyers, technology, and space. To fit the growth, they rented a big, fancy office in one of Miami's most prestigious neighborhoods. Dad's firm became one of the most successful boutique law firms in the country. Every year was better than the last.

But then the world changed. The economy recovered, and incoming cases were drying up, but the firm's size stayed the same. "You can't have all these lawyers sitting around doing nothing," Dad said. So he brought on new business partners who brought on new case work. "We took cases we didn't want to do but needed. We worked with cheapskate multinational corporations and some truly awful people."

Dad was realizing a big problem. Practicing law and running a law firm were totally different skill sets. "I was a great lawyer but a mediocre businessman," he said. "I was terrible at hiring. I brought on egotistical partners, incompetent managers, and mediocre lawyers. I gave work to people they never should have been doing. I had our human resources manager doing bookkeeping and accounting. Ridiculous! One employee embezzled a hundred thousand dollars from the firm that triggered a multiyear lawsuit."

Spoiler alert: Don't embezzle money from sophisticated attorneys.

The more the firm grew, the harder it was to keep everyone happy. "There's a reason they call lawyers sharks. Most are egotistical narcissists. Keeping five happy was easy. Keeping forty happy was a nightmare," Dad recalled.

Size turned small problems into big problems. "One time while working a high-stakes case, our office's internet went out. We had dozens of lawyers who couldn't work on the eve of a huge case. Only a miracle saved us. My nephew's dorky tech friend came in and slept in the office the whole weekend until all our internet problems were solved."

Cash flow was becoming a problem. "We had hundreds of thousands of dollars in monthly overhead." Worse, his firm had to fight hard to get paid. It turns out people love *not* paying their attorneys.

Speaking of cash, Dad was better with words than numbers. "I'm a freaking lawyer! I didn't know shit about budgeting or finances." The stakes were higher. Life was more expensive. One small house had become a big house and a vacation home. Hondas became BMWs. Elementary school tuition became private school and college tuition. He needed the firm to make more and more money to fund it all.

Running the firm took a lot out of him. Dad had to manage high-stakes lawsuits, dozens of employees, complex business-partner relationships, a relentless travel schedule, ballooning overhead, shrinking revenue, an expensive lifestyle, the looming possibility of bankruptcy, and financial ruin. "I created a monster. I was burning out mentally, emotionally, and physically. It was affecting everyone around me."

Dad hit his breaking point. Two decades after setting off on his own, he did the last—and only—thing he could do. He shut the firm down and returned to big corporate law. "We were victims of our own success. At the end of the day, all I really grew was headaches," Dad concluded.

Risk = Damage x Existence x Exposure

DAMAGE: WHAT'S AT STAKE?

Running a start-up is like chewing glass and staring into the abyss. After a while, you stop staring, but the glass chewing never ends.
—Elon Musk

Throughout this book, we've looked at everything through the "what if bad stuff happens" lens. Growth risk, the final risk, is about the inverse. What if good stuff happens?

Surviving means you get to grow. You can sell more stuff, hire more employees, impact more people, make more money, grow your confidence, earn more praise, and elevate your reputation. If you grow right, that is. Grow wrong, and this blessing may be a curse in disguise.

EXISTENCE: WHAT RISKS EXIST?

Like cancer, bad growth will create more bullshit than anything else. More fires to put out. More drama. More stress and burnout. More headaches and heartaches. Not only that, but growth raises the stakes. More can go right and wrong. There's more money to gain and lose and more people to satisfy and disappoint.

EXPOSURE: WHAT HAPPENS WHEN YOU GROW?

Growth is the ultimate stress test. It stresses *everything*. Size turns small problems into big problems. Subtle cracks become giant fissures. A strong foundation will support strong growth, while a weak one will crumble under growth's pressure.

Let's review. Growing will uncover the full spectrum of your industry's risks. As a bigger business, you'll become more sensitive to market, economic, and political shifts. Your business model will become more complicated the more people it has to satisfy. Growth will stress your relationships with your customers and clients when it comes at the cost of quality.

Growing means you won't be playing with amateurs anymore. Rivals will become more sophisticated and offer more compelling alternatives. You must resist the pull toward commoditization.

Marketing channels will have to pump more oxygen into the business. The more you rely on rented channels, the more fragile you will be. More products and services will complicate operations. You'll have more people to hire and more relationships to manage. Eventually your merry band of misfits will grow into a professionally staffed culture with characteristics you never planned for. What will you do when culture becomes cult?

Your small business tools might not be the right big business tools. Growth will attract more attention from cybercriminals. Success means jealous and malicious rivals will use the legal system against you. Contracts and taxes will become more complex. Lawsuits will become messier, more expensive, and more consequential. Growth means bigger and more complex numbers to keep track of. Growth may also mean growing expenses faster than revenue can handle.

More than anything else, growth will test you. Starting a small business and running a big one are totally different skill sets. If your ego grows faster than your capabilities, ambitions will mutate into delusions of grandeur. A bigger business may seem more successful on the surface but may just be a bigger ball and chain you can't step away from.

Success will tempt you into growing a lifestyle your business can't support. Growth will suck more time, money, and energy out of you. Growth will change your relationship with your business. Will you love your bigger business as much as you did the smaller version, or will it just pile your life with more bullshit?

GROWTH OPPORTUNITY

Growth has obvious benefits when it relates to more money. However, growth can also be treated as its own elegant risk design protocol. Growing into new markets is an opportunity to reduce your dependency on any single market. The right business model becomes stronger as it grows, as is the case with many community-oriented platforms. Creating new products with product-market fit ensures you'll always have ways to make money.

Adding new people spreads risk across more people and gives your business more intellectual resources. Streamlining operations with better technology reduces your reliance on people while boosting your operational capacity.

Opening new marketing channels ensures constant access to the people who pay you. More products and services make you more adaptable to shifting environments. More of the right people and tools will ensure things run smoothly. Making more money can build up your reserves so you can weather harsher storms.

CHOOSING GROWTH RISK

Growth is a choice. Just because you can grow doesn't mean you should grow. Seven years after closing down his firm to rejoin Big Law, Dad rebelled again. "I have to be on my own." Dad isn't built for big stuffy corporations. But this time he's doing it differently. "I'm going to stay small. I'll say no to whoever I want and only work on what I want," Dad promised himself.

TACO STREET AND GROWTH RISK

Taco Street was the best thing that ever happened to me. Before, I was aimlessly wandering and wondering if I had a role in "the real world." Today, I'm a successful entrepreneur and a wiser person. But once Taco Street stopped growing, it was a sign I stopped growing as an entrepreneur. It was a sign I needed to grow in another direction.

This book was my path to growth—not as an entrepreneur but as an author. Taco Street gave me the experience, desire, resources, time, and seemingly infinite firestorm of energy needed to create this book.

This book has been a worthy struggle. It challenged me like nothing else could. It radicalized how I think about business, what it means to survive, and it revealed me to myself. It changed the way I interface with reality and make decisions. It forced the deepest levels of introspection I've ever experienced and surfaced deep-rooted emotional tensions I'm now exploring in therapy.

I've realized that even as the author of this book, I am still very much a beginner on this journey I've laid out. I fall into the traps I've written about. I push glaring vulnerabilities out of my mind, hoping they'll disappear. I forget to go through the exercises I've described. I've just begun the process of applying these lessons to my personal life outside my business. But more and more, when I come across problems, I find myself returning to the lessons and frameworks I've already built.

My job is to find out how I will grow next. Until I do, Taco Street will continue to be my world-traveling bill-paying adventure buddy, shielding me from creditors, keeping me out of cubicles, and financing extra-guacamole-filled tacos.

KEY TAKEAWAYS

· Growth can be the best and worst thing to happen to your business.

· Growth is the ultimate stress test. It raises the stakes, exposes your relationship to your environment, and stresses every aspect inside your business—and most importantly, you.

· A well-designed business in the right environment will sustain growth.

· A poorly designed business in any environment will not.

- Like muscles, intelligent growth can make your business even more resilient.

- Growth is a choice. Just because you can grow doesn't mean you should grow.

- Grow wisely or don't grow at all.

CONCLUSION

Brad Larsen is (still) a doer. Life hasn't been easy for him after being unceremoniously exited from Float Temple, the business he started years earlier. He's been riding a roller coaster of emotions, relationships, finances, and uncertainty about where to go next.

Over lunch, I hesitate to ask the obvious question. "Have you thought about getting a job?"

In a flash, a fire in his eye sparks and spoils everything he's about to say. "Fuuuuuck no! I'm performing miracles out here!"

He shows me his new venture—a mobile personal training business. Inside the van he drives around town is something that looks like a futuristic leg-press machine attached to a computer. Compared to his old business, this one is much simpler. No business partners. No brick-and-mortar store. No government bureaucrats. No investors. No employees. Brad is on his own.

I give Brad's machine a spin. I jump in the van as he fires up both the machine and himself. He blasts dance music as I start leg-pressing with all the force I have. The machine pushes toward me, and I resist with everything I have. The cycle repeats a few more times. Brad is amped. "Push! Resist! You can do it! More power! One more rep! Hell Yeah!" I do the same cycle with bench press and rows. In fifteen minutes, I've gone through an entire strength routine. Exhausted, I give Brad a wobbly armed high five. I can see why he's excited.

Brad tells me about his other clients. He shows me a video of a geriatric man doing the same movements I just did. "This dude has Parkinson's disease! Before me, he was wheelchair bound. Now, for the first time in years, he's zipping around his house like a maniac. His kids couldn't believe what they're seeing." He tells me about another Parkinson's patient who can walk normally for the first time in years, and a recently divorced woman who's becoming physically strong and gaining confidence for the first time in her life.

He then tells me the craziest story. "One of my clients was flying with a friend in his small plane from Italy to Greece. The power steering gives out, and my guy has to manhandle the controls of his plane for four hours so he can land safely. He told me he never would have had the strength to pull it off if it weren't for this training. Two people would be fucking dead if it weren't for me!"

Brad is fired up. He doesn't know how or where he'll grow from here. All he knows is he's not tapping out. Brad Larsen the missionary, the creator, the hustler, the entrepreneur survives. Not because anyone lets him, but because he chooses to.

Entrepreneurship is a ridiculous proposition. You're betting that you can be one of the few who can build a life by creating a business that gives others what they want, all while adapting to a complex world outside your control. On this path is the very real chance you wind up financially ruined and emotionally traumatized.

But for you, the only proposition more ridiculous is not being an entrepreneur. So since you're going to be ridiculous, you might as well survive. Remember that survival is a choice. Every day you choose to be an entrepreneur, you make the choice to survive. Survival is about protecting the energy that makes you want to do it all in the first place.

Survival demands contending with risk. Risk is about understanding the world you do control so that you can better adapt to the world you don't. Survival means designing a resilient network of parts and forces capable of satisfying you and the people around you.

Most importantly, survival means looking at yourself. You are the ultimate risk to your business. Whether it lives, dies, or thrives is the consequence of your decisions. To survive, you must challenge your assumptions; reflect on your personality, tendencies, and competencies; and control your lifestyle. Survival means learning to see the world through rational frames while honoring the irrationalities of your emotions. Survival demands putting your business over your ego. Survival even means being prepared to end your business if that's what it takes for the entrepreneur inside of you to survive.

Surviving means you get to thrive. Surviving and thriving means learning to tightrope the tensions between risk and opportunity, certainty and doubt, optimism and pessimism, darkness and light. This is the core of entrepreneurship.

Thrive so you can effortlessly benefit from forces outside your control. Thrive so you can own a resilient asset that supports you and the people around you. Thrive so you can discover profitable and fulfilling expressions of your highest traits. Thrive so you can be not a character in but the author of your own story.

WHAT NOW?

Throughout the book, I listed many directives for you to explore the risks and opportunities hiding in your business and reflect on yourself. Go back and revisit your responses. Don't wait. Confront those risks, or reality will do it for you. Explore those opportunities, or they will pass you by. Pay attention to your newly developed risk senses, and apply the questions proposed by the RDEE formula to guide your next steps.

If you're looking for help connecting to risks and opportunities in your business, would like to share your own survival and/or disaster story, would like me to share my ideas with your team or audience, or would just like to say howdy, then contact me on my website: _survivalfirstbook.com_.

AFTERWORD

I was lounging in an apartment lobby, waiting to tour with my clients—something I'd done hundreds of times. A young apartment locator walked in with her clients. By her questions, I could tell she was new to the business.

If only she knew what I know, I mused. *She'd be making way more money, working her own hours, and traveling whenever she wanted.*

I almost facepalmed as my mind–light bulb lit up. *She* can *know what I know! I can make a course!* It was so obvious. I had the wisdom, experience, writing skills, tools, tricks of the trade, and success few could copy. My course would be amazing.

For the first time in a long time, my entrepreneur senses were tingling. Apartment locating was still a thriving industry. With a course, I wouldn't be limited to Texas. I could theoretically sell it in any city where apartment locating was a thing. I wouldn't have to deal with any pesky real estate bureaucracies either. After some quick research, I found ten cities I could sell to. It was a massive market.

The business model would be simple. Make a course. Sell it online. Profit. This course would give me an immediate and hard-to-replicate monopoly. Few had the success, authority, or skills to create what I could create. Larger locating companies whose models relied on their agents not going off on their own would never create a course like this. I would be a mentor guiding people to become the rebellious entrepreneur I was.

Unlike with Taco Street, I wouldn't be plugging into a business that already had product-market fit. I'd have to find it myself, but I suspected I could start somewhere close. Online real estate courses were a proven market. Apartment locating was a proven industry. Plenty of people were eager for the kind of success I had. All I would have to do was find the right product-market balance to bridge it all together.

As a product person, I knew building the course would be easy. All I had to do was repurpose everything I'd documented in Taco Street's Business Cookbook to turn it into a course. The tools seemed straightforward. There were plenty of simple course-building options to choose from. And I had plenty of friends with their own successful courses to learn from.

I'd have to get over some of my own mental blocks to market it. But oh boy, if I could nail it, the money would be really nice. Taco Street's operations were solid, but they don't scale far. With a digital product, I wouldn't need better operations. Information scales better than operations. Selling a hundred digital courses is infinitely easier than working with a hundred clients.

I wouldn't need many people to get the course off the ground. I knew I could do that part myself. After that, I wouldn't need more than a few project-based freelancers to take it to the next level. Protecting an online course legally would be new territory, but finding out how to do it didn't seem too hard. Most exciting, an online course could buy me passive income—the holy grail of cash flow. No working with clients. No cranking the wheel. No burnout. I could make money while I slept. With my belly fired up, I got to work and launched the course a few weeks later. A few weeks after that, I began a family trip to Spain. As we got off the plane, a notification bubbled up on my phone: *Somebody has bought your course. $1,500 will be deposited into your account in two to three business days.*

For the first time in a long time, I felt like an entrepreneur again.

ACKNOWLEDGMENTS

No one journeys alone.

To the people who trusted me to tell their stories, and to those who shared theirs with the world: Brad Larsen, Rudy Delgado, Zach Horvath, Michael Kane, Malcolm Bradford, Jordan Bishop, Lukas Wells, Drew Binsky, Joe Speiser, Jesse Cole, Carl Gorman, Matt Landau, Tucker Max, Niko Velikov, Oscar Gil, Shaun Offenbach, Stas Bilder, Hillarie Rose, Bryan Dagle, and Stephanie Martinez.

To the All-Star Team who helped me turn digital word vomit into a real and beautiful book: Mark Chait, Rebecca Pillsbury, Chas Hoppe, Amanda Hoppe, Emily Gindlesparger, Hussein Al-Baiaty, AJ Hendrickson, Gunnar Rogers, Kacy Wren, Rose Friel, Michael Nagin, Danielle Quisenberry-Ruvolo, Lynne Lennon, John van der Woude, and Tara Taylor.

To my team at Taco Street for doing great work and helping me carve out the time to write this book: Whitney Turcic, Adela Fuentes, Joyce Galicia, Caihza Nini, and Rabbi Hassan.

To those who gave me love and inspiration, contributed to the ideas in this book, and suffered my long yet endearing rants: Imran Walij, Andrew Jacobs, Edgar Galindo, Edgar Gutierrez, Vignesh Jeyaraman, Mauricio Galarce, Fabio Galarce, Yash Chitneni, Michelle Rivera, Ricky Pooler, Alexander Rojas, Lauren Knight-Hughes, Hallie Knight-Hughes, Michael Cedeno, Jack Kelly, Brittany Weltner, Dave Nuzzolo, Megan Robitaille, Melanie Pellman, Brice Gump, Robbie Thomas, Conor Hall, Leanne Valenti, Nate Eckman, Zachary Hanson, Andy Kalt, Derek Varona, Daniel Florencio, Hutch Herchenbach, Lindsey Payton, Quoc Anh Tran, Dani Smith, Max Benson, and Matt Felser.

To Nassim Taleb and Daniel Kahneman, whose work influenced me to explore the subject of risk. To East Austin, whose charming streets I strolled for countless hours during the pandemic while the ideas for this book began to blossom. To my gym, Squatch Frontier Fitness, for being my daily sanctuary. To any creator of the hyperspecific musical subgenre of atmospheric dub techno whose calmly hypnotic sounds coated my ears for hundreds of hours as I worked on this book.

And lastly, of course, to my dad, mom, sister, and abuela.

THE APPENDIX, A.K.A. THE RISKPENDIX

Below is a collection of words and concepts I've described throughout the book. Return to this section if you want a quick refresher on what you learned.

CHAPTER 2: RISK AND OPPORTUNITY

- **Risk:** Potential bad stuff.
- **Potential:** Stuff we don't know will happen.
- **Bad:** Stuff we don't want to happen.
- **Stuff (a.k.a. Survival):** What makes us continue to choose entrepreneurship.
- **Opportunity:** Potential good stuff.
- **Survival:** The money, time, and energy needed for you to continue choosing entrepreneurship.
- **Money:** The income you need to make to continue on.
- **Time:** The hours required to run your business.
- **Energy:** The logical and emotional reasons that make you choose entrepreneurship.

CHAPTER 3: SENSING RISK

- **Risk Blindness:** When how we feel about risk doesn't match reality.
- **Opportunity Blindness:** When how we feel about opportunity doesn't match reality.
- **The Risk Sense:** The ability to rationally process and emotionally connect to risk.
- **The RDEE Formula:** Risk = Damage x Existence x Exposure
- **Risk:** Potential bad stuff.
- **Damage:** The potential negative effects of the risk happening.
- **Existence:** If the risk exists or not.
- **Exposure:** The likelihood the risk happens.

CHAPTER 4: BECOMING A RISK SOMMELIER

- **Risk Sommelier:** Somebody with masterfully attuned risk senses.
- **Risk Flavors:** Different ways risks and opportunities manifest in the real world.
- **Ordinary Risk:** Bad stuff you can imagine happening.
- **Ordinary Opportunity:** Good stuff you can imagine happening.
- **Black Swan Risk:** Bad stuff you never imagined happening.
- **Black Swan Opportunity:** Good stuff you never imagined happening.
- **Domino Risk:** Bad stuff that follows other bad stuff happening.
- **Domino Opportunity:** Good stuff that follows other good stuff happening.
- **Compound Risk (a.k.a. Death by a Thousand Risks):** Lots of different bad stuff happening at the same time.
- **Compound Opportunity:** Lots of good stuff happening at the same time.
- **Transfer Risk:** When you adopt third-party problems (your clients' problems become your problems).
- **Transfer Opportunity:** When you adopt third-party opportunities (e.g., your clients making more money means they can pay you more).
- **Timing Risk:** How consequences are magnified when bad stuff happens.
- **Timing Opportunity:** How upsides are magnified when good stuff happens.
- **Concentration Risk:** When a single bad thing happening has large consequences.
- **Concentration Opportunity:** When a single good thing happening has a high upside.
- **Middle Risk:** When the danger lies in between the extremes (e.g., being in a boring relationship with your business).
- **Middle Opportunity:** When good stuff happens from blending opposing forces (e.g., combining product-oriented people with market-oriented people).

CHAPTER 5: WHAT TO DO ABOUT RISK

- **Choosing Risk:** The network of choices responsible for the problems and opportunities you're exposed to.
- **Risk Design Protocols:** Ways you can design or redesign your business to give you better sets of risks and opportunities.
- **Simplify:** Reduce the number of ways things can go wrong.
- **Alexander's Law:** Things that can't go wrong won't go wrong.
- **Diversify:** Increase the number of things that have to go wrong for you to be affected.
- **Backups:** Extra layers of protection to defend against bad stuff happening.
- **The Happy Hour Pivot:** Slightly changing how you do business to change the risks and opportunities you're exposed to.

CHAPTER 6: INDUSTRY RISK

- **Industry Risk:** The unavoidable risks you inherit by being in your business.
- **Industry Opportunity:** The upsides you're exposed to by being in your business.
- **The Lindy Effect (a.k.a. the Reverse Aging Principle):** The older something is, the longer it will likely continue to exist.
- **Kiddie Poolers:** People who methodically research and gradually make their way into the unknown.
- **Pacific Oceaners:** People who decide to do something and figure things out as they go.

CHAPTER 7: MARKET RISK

- **Markets:** The series of inputs needed to make what you sell (supply) along with the people you sell to (demand).
- **Market Risk:** Whatever makes your business climate less habitable.
- **Market Opportunity:** Whatever makes it cheaper to run your business or increases the demand for what you sell.

- **Small Slice:** When your business needs a small portion of a large market to survive.
- **Big Slice:** When your business needs a big portion of a small market to survive.

CHAPTER 8: ECONOMIC RISK

- **Economic Risk:** When the people you rely on to have money have less of it.
- **Economic Opportunity:** When the people you rely on to have money have more of it.
- **Necessity:** Stuff people need (e.g., rent).
- **Luxury:** Stuff people don't need (e.g., Gucci purses).
- **Budget Load:** The percent of somebody's income they spend on your product.

CHAPTER 9: POLITICAL RISK

- **Political Risk:** Rule changes that make your environment less habitable.
- **Political Opportunity:** Rule changes that introduce new or simpler ways of doing business.
- **Simulation ~~Theory~~ Fact:** The reality that people and institutions regularly manipulate your external environment.

CHAPTER 10: BUSINESS MODEL RISK

- **Business Model:** The network of incentives between you, the people you work with, and the people who pay you.
- **Business Model Risk:** When your business model stops working for you, the people you work with, or the people who pay you.
- **Business Model Opportunity:** Finding new ways to align incentives with new people.
- **Schemer:** Somebody who makes their business model work for themselves but not others.
- **Martyr:** Somebody who makes their business model work for

everyone but themselves.

CHAPTER 11: PRODUCT-MARKET FIT RISK

- **Product-Market Fit Risk:** When people (the market) don't buy what you're selling (the product).
- **Product-Market Fit Opportunity:** When you create new ways to make money by selling something people want.
- **Product Person:** Somebody who focuses more on making than selling.
- **Market Person:** Somebody who focuses more on selling than making.

CHAPTER 12: "COMPETITIVE" RISK

- **Replacement Risk (not competitive risk):** When people replace your business with another product or service.
- **Replacement Opportunity:** When you no longer have to struggle to differentiate yourself.
- **Direct Replacement:** Other similar people or companies that clients might choose over you (e.g., Netflix versus Hulu).
- **Indirect Replacement:** Unsimilar people or companies that clients might choose over you (e.g., Netflix versus bars).
- **Commodity:** Something infinitely replaceable, distinguishable only by price.
- **Monopoly:** Something irreplaceable.

CHAPTER 13: MARKETING RISK

- **Marketing Channel:** Where you connect to the people who pay you (e.g., social media, networking events, flyers, etc.).
- **Marketing Risk:** When you get cut off from your market.
- **Marketing Opportunity:** Finding new ways and places to connect with the people that give you money.
- **Crackhead Marketing:** When your business is overly dependent on powerful but fickle marketing channels.
- **Rented Channels:** Marketing channels others own and control.
- **Owned Channels:** Marketing channels you own and control.

CHAPTER 14: OPERATIONS RISK

- **Operations:** The network of solutions that solve incoming problems.
- **Operations Risk:** When you can't solve enough incoming problems.
- **Operations Opportunity:** When your increased ability to solve problems leads to more money, time, and energy.
- **The Lucy Ratio:** The ratio of incoming problems over problem-solving capacity.

CHAPTER 15: PRODUCT RISK

- **Product Risk:** When you can't solve incoming problems around your product or service.
- **The Cheesecake Factory Problem:** When you overload your operations with the volume and variety of problems to solve.

CHAPTER 16: PEOPLE RISK

- **The Swiss Army Knife Problem:** When too much of your operations relies on a single person.
- **People Risk:** When people who work with you stop working with you.
- **Rented Knowledge:** The knowledge it takes to run your business that lives outside the business.
- **Owned Knowledge:** The knowledge it takes to run your business that lives inside the business.
- **The Business Cookbook:** The collection of documented knowledge required to run your business.

CHAPTER 17: TECHNOLOGY RISK

- **Technology Risk:** When the tools you use to run your business stop working.
- **Technology Opportunity:** Finding new tools that make doing business cheaper and more efficient.
- **Technology Stack:** The combined set of tools you use to run your business.

CHAPTER 18: CYBERSECURITY RISK

- **Cybersecurity Risk:** When you get hacked or are the target of cyber-crime.
- **Cybersecurity Opportunity:** Gaining peace of mind by lowering the odds you get hacked.
- **Password Check:** A quick process that scans your stored passwords for overall security.
- **Password Manager:** A place to store and create scrambled passwords.
- **Digital Footprint:** The number of online locations your information is stored.
- **Multifactor Authentication:** Backup verification protocols that ensure you are the one accessing your own accounts.

CHAPTER 19: LEGAL RISK

- **Legal Risk:** When somebody uses the legal system against you.
- **Legal Opportunity:** Decreasing the stress of legal conflict and finding new ways to make or save money.
- **Bullies:** People who abuse the legal system to attack rivals.
- **Trolls:** Pond-scum losers whose businesses revolve around using the legal system to effectively extort money from others.
- **Sharkiness:** The degree to which people like to engage in legal conflicts.
- **Corporate Structures:** Legal entities you can create to shield yourself from personal liability.
- **Mediation:** Where you bring your case to a neutral judge who recommends a legally nonbinding resolution.
- **Arbitration:** Like mediation, but where the resolutions of the arbitrators (also known as a private judge) are binding.
- **Litigation:** All-out legal warfare.

CHAPTER 20: MONEY RISK

- **Money Risk:** When you run out of funding for your business.
- **Money Opportunity:** When you find better ways to create revenue or manage expenses.

- **Margins:** The difference between how much money you make and how much you spend.
- **Cost Flexibility:** The degree to which your costs can be changed.
- **Density:** How big transactions are in relation to your total revenue.
- **Where's My Fucking Money Risk:** When you have to fight to get paid.
- **Whoops I Lost Your Money Risk:** When you can't deliver the products, events, or services you've already collected money for.
- **Seasonality:** The degree to which your revenue is concentrated in certain times of the year.

CHAPTER 21: COMPETENCY RISK

- **The Ego Problem:** The tension between satisfying your ego and doing what's best for your business.
- **Competency Risk:** When you screw up the work you do.
- **Competency Opportunity:** When you increase the number or complexity of problems your business can solve by making yourself smarter or hiring smarter people.

CHAPTER 22: ABSENTEE RISK

- **Absentee Risk:** What happens to your business when you unexpectedly leave it.
- **Absentee Opportunity:** The money, time, and energy you can save by making your business less reliant on you.
- **Outsourcerer:** Somebody who is skilled at getting others to do work for them.
- **Control Freak:** Somebody who loves doing everything themselves.
- **Cat-Like Business:** A business that does just fine without you.
- **Dog-Like Business:** A business that does not do well without you.
- **Location Stress Test:** Seeing how long you can be in different locations before your business is affected.
- **Time Stress Test:** Seeing how long you can stop working before your business is affected.

CHAPTER 23: VAMPIRE RISK

- **Vampire Risk:** When you take too much money from your business.
- **Vampire Opportunity:** The high investment returns you can get by investing in your business.
- **Vampire's Death Spiral:** When draining your business's resources speeds its downfall.
- **Vampire:** Somebody who takes too much money from their business.
- **Investor:** Somebody who puts money back into their business.

CHAPTER 24: BURNOUT RISK

- **Burnout Risk:** The ripple effects on your personal and professional life when you run out of energy.
- **Burnout Opportunity:** All of the ways you can improve your life by protecting your time and energy.
- **Fast Burn:** When you use too much energy too quickly.
- **Slow Burn:** When you gradually lose energy over a long period of time.
- **Extremist:** Somebody who tends to go all in with anything they do.
- **Balanced:** Somebody who reserves energy for themselves.

CHAPTER 25: RELATIONSHIP RISK

- **Relationship Risk:** When your relationship with your business becomes one you don't want anymore.
- **Relationship Opportunity:** When you have an amazing relationship with your business that gives you much more than what you put in.
- **Situationship:** An undefined relationship that takes on forms nobody wants.
- **Hyperobsessive Relationship:** When your business consumes all your energy at the expense of the rest of your life.
- **Toxic Relationship:** When you hate your business but can't step away from it.
- **Boring Relationship:** When you don't hate your business enough to end it but don't love it enough to give it more energy than you have to.

Milton Keynes UK
Ingram Content Group UK Ltd.
UKHW010631280424
441851UK00011B/155/J

9 798989 938520